REDUCED GRADIENT BUBBLE MODEL IN DEPTH

REDUCED GRADIENT BUBBLE MODEL IN DEPTH

BRUCE R. WIENKE

BEST PUBLISHING COMPANY

"All models are wrong, but some are useful."
Los Alamos National Laboratory Thermonuclear Simulations Group
September 20, 1972

Design by: Jill McAdoo
Edited by: James T. Joiner

Copyright © 2003 by Best Publishing Company

All rights reserved

No part of this book may be reproduced, stored in a retrieval system, or transmitted in any form or by any means, electronic, mechanical, photocopying, microfilming, recording, or otherwise, without written permission from the publisher.

ISBN: 1-930536-11-9
Library of Congress Catalog Card Number: 2002116450

Best Publishing Company
PO Box 30100
Flagstaff, AZ 86003-0100

www.bestpub.com

· TABLE OF CONTENTS ·

PREFACE	**VII**
AUTHOR SKETCH	**IX**
UNITS AND EQUIVALENCIES	**XI**
INTRODUCTION	**1**
Diving Phase Dynamics ·	2
COMPUTATIONAL SYNTHESIS	**3**
RGBM Motivation and Implementations ·	3
RGBM Underpinnings ·	5
Inert and Metabolic Gas Transport ·	7
Bubbles ·	8
Temperature ·	11
Bubble Seeds ·	12
Slow Tissue Compartments ·	13
Venous Gas Emboli ·	14
Multidiving ·	15
Adaptation ·	16
MATERIAL DYNAMICS	**17**
Surface Tension ·	17
Surfactants ·	19
Compressibility and Cubical Expansion ·	20
Bubble Metrics ·	21
Seed Material Response ·	22
CRITICAL PHASE VOLUME LIMIT	**25**
Phase Exposure Integral ·	25
Repetitive Exposures ·	26
RGBM MODEL IMPLEMENTATIONS	**29**
Iterative RGBM Implementation ·	29
Folded RGBM Implementation ·	33

RESULTS AND COMPARISONS   40
Nonstop Comparisons • **40**
Deep Comparisons • **43**
Helium Comparisons • **43**
Gradient Factor Comparisons • **44**
Reverse Profile Comparisons • **48**
Extreme Diving Comparisons • **53**
EOS Comparisons • **53**

DEEP STOPS AND HELIUM   56
Deep Stop Strategies • **57**
Deep Stop Models • **60**
Laboratory Experiments • **61**
Helium Strategies • **62**
Helium Dynamics • **64**

RISK ANALYSIS AND VALIDATION   66
Risk Estimators • **66**
RGBM Profile Risks • **67**
RGBM Profile Data Bank • **70**
RGBM Field Testing • **70**

SUMMARY   73

APPENDIX   77

REFERENCES   87

· PREFACE ·

This exposition links phase mechanics to decompression theory with equations and corresponding dialogue. Theory and application are, at times, more artform than exact science. Some believe deterministic modeling is only fortuitous. Technological advance, elucidation of competing mechanisms, and resolution of model issues over the past 90 years has not been rapid. Model applications tend to be *ad hoc*, tied to data fits, and difficult to quantify on first principles. Almost any description of decompression processes in tissue and blood can be disputed, and possibly turned around on itself. The fact that decompression sickness occurs in metabolic and perfused matter makes it difficult to design and analyze experiments outside living matter. Yet, for application to safe diving, we need models to build tables and meters. And, regardless of biological complexity, certain coarse grain physics principles, often neglected in the past, are making a substantial change in diver staging regimens, decompression theory, and coupled data analysis. Happily today, we are looking at both dissolved gases and bubbles in our staging regimens, and not just the dissolved gas approach of Haldane which has been an icon for the past century.

The reader will notice an emphasis on free gas phases (bubbles, nuclei, and whatever else is not dissolved), and comments about free phase models versus (just) dissolved phase models, the present basis for most decompression analysis. Most comments are based on recent experiments coupled with basic physics. While we do not know all the facts yet, many take the view that phase models correlated with available data, linked to underlying physical principles, and which recover dissolved gas models in appropriate limits, are the types of models which which should be extended, refined, and used in table and meter algorithms. Coupled to model algorithms are statistical analyses of decompression risk data, folded into meaningful and useful table and meter format, an area under active study. Models such as the RGBM have already gained widespread popularity, acceptance, and growth in prominence, particularly in the deep, decompression, and mixed gas sectors. This is due to released Tables, meter implementations, computer software, and wholesale positive results and feedback by real divers across all venues. Some have called it a revolution in diving.

The intent here is to present a working view of physical phase mechanics, followed by application to decompression theory in diving, mostly focusing on theory with application, including equations. The discussion is neither a medical nor physiological synthesis. Such aspects are simplified, and for some certainly oversimplified. Nonetheless, it is directed toward the diver and reader with some rudimentary understanding of decompression. Background in the physical or life sciences is helpful, but certainly not requisite. Basically, the mechanistics of tissue gas exchange, bubbles and nucleation, supersaturation, perfusion and diffusion, and related mechanisms are discussed.

The physics, biology, engineering, physiology, medicine, and chemistry of diving center on pressure, and pressure changes. The average individual is subject to atmospheric pressure swings of 3% at sea level, as much as 20% a mile in elevation, more at higher altitudes, and all usually over time spans of hours to days. Divers and their equipment can experience compressions and decompressions orders of magnitude greater, and within considerably shorter time scales. While effects of pressure change are readily quantified in physics, chemistry, and engineering applications, the physiology, medicine, and biology of pressure changes in living systems are much more complicated. Caution is needed in transposing biological principles from one pressure range to another. Incomplete knowledge and mathematical complexities often prevent extensions of even simple causal relationships in biological science. Causal relationships between observables are, of course, the pervue of physics, and that difficult process in living systems is biophysics. Other source material and further development can be found in the References.

Material detailed builds upon and extends topics presented in *Physics, Physiology, and Decompression Theory for the Technical and Commercial Diver*, *Basic Diving Physics and Application*, *Diving above Sea Level*, *High Altitude Diving*, *Basic Decompression Theory and Application*, *Technical Diving in Depth*, as referenced in the text.

Thanks again to colleagues and friends in the diving community, copiously listed in all other monographs and publications. Special thanks to Jim Joiner and Jill McAdoo at Best Publishing for their help and sharp eyes in manuscript translation and book preparation.

Tim O'Leary, Director, NAUI Technical Diving Operations, has been a prime mover for RGBM testing, validation, Table fabrication, and data collection. His contributions to the successes of RGBM are legion. Thank you, Buddy. And NAUI too.

And warm thanks to Kyle Denman.

Good reading and good diving.

· AUTHOR SKETCH ·

Bruce Wienke is a Program Manager in the Nuclear Weapons Technology/Simulation and Computing Office at the Los Alamos National Laboratory (LANL), with interests in computational decompression and models, gas transport, and phase mechanics. He contributes to underwater symposia, educational publications, technical periodicals, and decompression workshops, having authored seven monographs (*Technical Diving in Depth, Decompression Theory, Physics, Physiology and Decompression Theory for the Technical and Commercial Diver, High Altitude Diving, Basic Diving Physics and Application, Diving Above Sea Level, Basic Decompression Theory and Application*) and some 200 technical journal articles. Diving environs include the Caribbean, South Pacific, Asia, inland and coastal United States, Hawaii, and polar Arctic and Antarctic for sundry technical, scientific, military, and recreational activities.

He functions on the LANL Nuclear Emergency Strategy Team (NEST), in exercises often involving Special Warfare Units, above and below water. He heads Southwest Enterprises, a consulting company for research and applications in overlapping areas of applied science and simulation, and functions as an Expert Witness in diving litigation.

Wienke is an Instructor Trainer/Technical Instructor with the National Association of Underwater Instructors (NAUI), serves on the Board of Directors (Vice Chairman for Technical Diving, Technical and Decompression Review Board Member), is a Master Instructor with the Professional Association of Diving Instructors (PADI) in various capacities (Instructor Review Committee), is an Institute Director with the YMCA, and is an Instructor Trainer/Technical Instructor with Scuba Diving International/Technical Diving International (SDI/TDI). His wintertime hobbies include skiing, coaching, and teaching as a Racing Coach and Instructor. He is certified with the United States Ski Coaches Association (USSCA) and Professional Ski Instructors of America (PSIA), and races in the United States Ski Association (USSA) Masters Series Competition, holding an 8 NASTAR racing handicap. Other interests include tennis, windsurfing, and mountain biking. He quarterbacked the '63 Northern Michigan Wildcats to an NCAA II Championship (Hickory Bowl).

Wienke received a B.S. in physics and mathematics from Northern Michigan University, M.S. in nuclear physics from Marquette University, and Ph.D. in particle physics from Northwestern University.

He belongs to the American Physical Society (APS), American Nuclear Society (ANS), Society of Industrial and Applied Mathematics (SIAM), South Pacific Underwater Medical Society (SPUMS), Undersea and Hyperbaric Medical Society (UHMS), and American Academy of Underwater Sciences (AAUS). He is a Fellow of the American Physical Society, and a Technical Committee Member of the American Nuclear Society.

Wienke, a former dive shop owner in Santa Fe, presently serves as a Consultant for decompression algorithms in the Industry. He has worked with DAN on applications of high performance computing and communications to diving, and is a Regional Data Coordinator for Project Dive Exploration. Scubapro, Suunto, Mares, Zeagle, HydroSpace, Plexus, Abysmal Diving, and Atomic Aquatics engage him (or have) as Consultant for meter algorithms. He is the developer of the Reduced Gradient Bubble Model (RGBM), a dual phase approach to staging diver ascents over an extended range of diving applications (altitude, nonstop, decompression, multiday, repetitive, multilevel, mixed gas, and saturation). A number of dive computers (Suunto, Mares, Plexus, HydroSpace, and others coming online) incorporate the modified and full iterative RGBM into staging regimens for technical and recreational diving. Aggressive computers with RGBM for helitrox, trimix, heliox, nitrox, air, and combinations are in the pipeline. GAP and ABYSS, commercial software products, feature some of the RGBM dynamical diving algorithms developed by him for Internet users and technical divers. The EXPLORER is a recently released full up RGBM computer for mixed gases, deco, and constant ppO_2 diving.

Wienke is also Associate Editor for the *International Journal of Aquatic Research and Education*, and is a former Contributing Editor of *Sources*, the NAUI Training Publication. NAUI Technical Training has adopted the RGBM for technical and recreational training, and employs RGBM trimix, heliair, nitrox, and air tables. Wienke is a Contributing Editor of *Advanced Diver* magazine.

· UNITS AND EQUIVALENCIES ·

Standard (SI) and English units are employed. By convention, by usage, or for ease, some nonstandard units are employed. Pressure and depth are both measured in feet of sea water (*fsw*) and meters of sea water (*msw*), with 1 *atm* = 33 *fsw* = 10 *msw* to good approximation. Specific densities, η (dimensionless), in pressure relationships are normalized to sea water density.

TIME
    1 megahertz = 10^6 *hertz* = 10^6 *sec*$^{-1}$

LENGTH
    1 m = *3.28 ft* = *1.09 yd* = *39.37 in*
    1 μm = 10^4 *angstrom* = 10^3 *nm* = 10^{-6} *m*
    1 km = *.62 mile*
    1 fathom = *6 ft*
    1 nautical mile = *6,080 ft* = *1.15 mile* = *1.85 km*
    1 light year = *9.46 x 10^{12} km* = *5.88 x 10^{12} mile*

SPEED
    1 km/hr = *27.77 cm/sec*
    1 mile/hr = *5,280 ft/sec*
    1 knot = *1.15 mi/hr* = *51.48 cm/sec*

VOLUME
    1 cm^3 = *.06 in^3*
    1 m^3 = *35.32 ft^3* = *1.31 yd^3*
    1 l = 10^3 *cm^3* = *.04 ft^3* = *1.05 qt*

MASS AND DENSITY
    1 g = *.04 oz*
    1 kg = *32.27 oz* = *2.20 lb*
    1 g/cm^3 = *.57 oz/in^3*
    1 kg/m^3 = *.06 lb/ft^3*

Force and Pressure

1 newton = 10^5 dyne = .22 lb
1 g/cm² = .23 oz/in²
1 kg/m² = .20 lb/ft²
1 atm = 33 fsw = 10 msw = 1.03 kg/cm² = 14.69 lbs/in²

Energy and Power

1 cal = 4.19 joule = 3.96 x 10^{-3} btu = 3.09 ft lb
1 joule = 10^7 ergs = .74 ft lb
1 keV = 10^3 eV = 1.60 x 10^{-16} joule
1 amu = 931.1 MeV
1 watt = 3.41 btu/hr = 1.34 x 10^{-3} hp

Electricity and Magnetism

1 coul = 2.99 x 10^9 esu
1 amp = 1 coul/sec = 1 volt/ohm
1 volt = 1 newton coul m = 1 joule/coul
1 gauss = 10^{-4} weber/m² = 10^{-4} newton/amp m
1 f = 1 coul/volt

Standard mathematical and physical conventions are followed. Bold face quantities are vectors, while roman face quantities are scalars. Fundamental constants are tabulated below. Full discussion of constants and impacts can be found in the References, particularly the physics and chemistry entries.

g_0 = 9.80 m/sec²   (Sea Level Acceleration of Gravity)
G_0 = 6.67 x 10^{-11} newton m² /kg²   (Gravitational Constant)
M_0 = 5.98 x 10^{24} kg   (Earth Mass)
Γ_0 = 1.98 cal/min cm²   (Solar Constant)
c = 2.998 x 10^8 m/sec   (Speed Of Light)
h = 6.625 x 10^{-34} joule sec   (Planck Constant)
R = 8.317 joule/gmole K°   (Universal Gas Constant)
k = 1.38 x 10^{-23} joule/gmole K°   (Boltzmann Constant)
N_0 = 6.025 x 10^{23} atoms/gmole   (Avogadro Number)
m_0 = 9.108 x 10^{-31} kg   (Electron Mass)
e_0 = 1.609 x 10^{-19} coulomb   (Electron Charge)
r_0 = .528 angstrom   (First Bohr Orbit)
ε_0 = $(4\pi)^{-1}$ x 1.11 x 10^{-10} f/m   (Vacuum Permittivity)

$\mu_0 = 4\pi \times 10^{-7}$ h/m (Vacuum Permeability)
$\kappa_0 = (4\pi \varepsilon_0)^{-1} = 8.91 \times 10^9$ m/f (Coulomb Constant)
$\alpha_0 = \mu_0/4\pi = 1 \times 10^{-7}$ h/m (Ampere Constant)
$\sigma_0 = 5.67 \times 10^{-8}$ watt/m² K°⁴ (Stefan-Boltzmann Constant)

Metrology is the science of measurement, and broadly construed, encompasses the bulk of experimental science. In the more restricted sense, metrology refers to the maintenance and dissemination of a consistent set of units, support for enforcement of equity in trade by weights and measure laws, and process control for manufacturing.

A measurement is a series of manipulations of physical objects or systems according to experimental protocols producing a number. The objects or systems involved are test objects, measuring devices, or computational operations. The objects and devices exist in and are influenced by some environment. The number relates to some unique feature of the object, such as the magnitude, or the intensity, or the weight, or time duration. The number is acquired to form the basis of decisions effecting some human feature or goal depending on the test object.

In order to attain the goal of useful decision, metrology requires that the number obtained is functionally identical whenever and wherever the measurement process is performed. Such a universally reproducible measurement is called a *proper measurement* and leads to describing *proper quantities*. The equivalences above relate *proper quantities* and the fundamental constants permit closure of physical laws. Unit conversion follows via the chain rule, where the identities listed define equivalence ratios that work like simple arithmetic fractions as far as unit conversions are concerned. Units cancel just like numbers.

• INTRODUCTION •

Diving models address the coupled issues of gas uptake and elimination, bubbles, and pressure changes in numerous computational frameworks. Application of a computational model to staging divers is called a diving algorithm. The reduced gradient bubble model (RGBM) is a modern one, treating the many facets of gas dynamics in tissue and blood consistently. Though the systematics of gas exchange, nucleation, bubble growth or collapse, and decompression are so complicated that theories only reflect pieces of the decompression sickness (DCS) puzzle, the risk and DCS statistics of staging algorithms can be easily collected and analyzed. And the record of the RGBM, just over the past five years or so, has been spectacular, especially so far as safe staging coupled to deep stops with overall shorter decompression times. And the dynamics port naturally to low risk recreational diving, with a major diver training agency, the National Association of Underwater Instructors (NAUI), releasing sets of air and nitrox Tables for sea level to altitudes of 10,000 *ft*. Also, a massive 600-page set of RGBM Tables (nitrox, heliox, trimix, helitrox, and constant oxygen partial pressure) is near completion and release for technical, mixed gas, extended range, and decompression diving, again, from sea level to 10,000 *ft* elevation. The structure and record of the RGBM embrace both, a truly modern model that is both useful and safe. Additionally the RGBM has been encoded in Suunto, Mares, Zeagle, Plexus, and Hydrospace decompression meters for air, nitrox, and mixed gases, exhibiting a fine safety record over many 100,000s of dives. GAP and ABYSS, software packages for divers, offer the RGBM as a major decompression management tool and staging protocol. The HydroSpace EXPLORER is the first full up RGBM computer incorporating deep stops, mixed gases, decompression and extended range, and altitude. Expect other meter manufacturers to follow suit in the not-so-distant future. An RGBM Data Bank has also been established for technical diving.

A set of recreational RGBM Tables (air and nitrox), 0 - 10,000 *feet* elevation, and directions for use, is also appended (before References).

We discuss the RGBM model, its basis, applications, validity, and testing. The last two are important. Models are one thing, even with all correct biophysics, and actual diving and testing are something else.

DIVING PHASE DYNAMICS

Under compression-decompression (divers, aviators), the body experiences many physical and biochemical changes, linked to differences between external pressures and internal dissolved and free gas partial pressures. Differences in pressures (gradients) drive gas transfer, fuel bubble growth, build supersaturation in tissues and blood, and spawn fluid flow. Gas exchange, bubble formation and elimination, and effects on and in blood and tissues are governed by many factors, such as diffusion, perfusion, phase separation and equilibration, nucleation and cavitation, local fluid shifts, and combinations thereof. Owing to the complexity of biological systems, multiplicity of tissues and media, diversity of interfaces and boundary conditions, and plethora of bubble impacting physical and chemical mechanisms, it is difficult to solve the decompression problem *in vivo*.

Early decompression studies adopted the supersaturation viewpoint. Closer looks at the physics of phase separation and bubbles in the mid-1970s, and insights into gas transfer mechanisms, culminated in extended kinetics and dissolved-free phase theories. Integration of both approaches can proceed on the numerical side because calculational techniques can be made equivalent. Phase and bubble models are more general than supersaturation models, incorporating their predictive capabilities as subsets. Statistical models, developed mostly in the mid-1980s, are gray from mechanistic viewpoint, but offer correlations with actual experiments and exposures, possibly the best approach to table fabrication.

Computational models gain efficacy by their ability to track data, often independently of physical interpretation. In that sense, the bottom line for computational models is utility, operational reliability, and reproducibility. Correct models can achieve such ends, but almost any model with sufficient parameter latitude could achieve those same ends. It is fair to say that deterministic models admit varying degrees of computational license, that model parameters may not correlate as complete set with the real world, and that not all mechanisms are addressed optimally. That is, perhaps, one reason why we see representative diving sectors, such as sport, military, commercial, and research, employing different tables, meters, models, and algorithms. Yet, given this situation, phase models attempting to treat both free and dissolved gas exchange, bubbles and gas nuclei, and free phase trigger points appear preferable to other flags. Phase models have the right physical signatures, and thus the potential to extrapolate reasonably when confronting new applications and data. So consider next the reduced gradient bubble model (RGBM), one very popular and successful dual phase diving model, both on fundamental physical bases and wideband diving applications in the future.

• COMPUTATIONAL SYNTHESIS •

The RGBM grew from needs of technical divers to more efficiently stage ascents consistent with coarse grain dissolved gas and bubble dynamics, and not just dissolved gas (Haldane) constraints. The depth, diversity, mix variation, and self consistency of RGBM diving applicability has satisfied that need. And safely.

The RGBM has gained tremendous popularity in the recreational and technical diving worlds in just the past two to three years, due to meter implementations, Internet software packages, specialized Table releases, technical word of mouth, NAUI training testing and adoption, Internet traffic, chamber tests, and, most of all, actual technical and recreational RGBM diving and validation. And the technical reasons are fairly clear.

RGBM Motivation And Implementations

Present notions of nucleation and bubbles suggest that decompression phase separation is random, yet highly probable, in body tissue. Once established, a gaseous phase will further grow by acquiring gas from adjacent saturated tissue, according to the strength of the free-dissolved gradient. Although exchange mechanisms are better understood, nucleation and stabilization mechanisms remain less so, and calculationally elusive. But even with a paucity of knowledge, many feel that existing practices and recent studies on bubbles and nuclei shed considerable light on growth and elimination processes and time scales. Their consistency with underlying physical principles suggest directions for table and meter modeling, beyond parameter fitting and extrapolation techniques. Recovering dissolved gas algorithms for short exposure times, phase models link to bubble mechanics and critical volume trigger points. The RGBM incorporates all of the above in all implementations, and additionally supports the efficacy of recently suggested safe diving practices, by simple virtue of its dual phase mechanics:

1. reduced nonstop time limits;
2. safety stops (or shallow swimming ascents) in the 10 - 20 *fsw* zone;
3. ascent rates not exceeding 30 *fsw/min*;
4. restricted repetitive exposures, particularly beyond 100 *fsw*;

5. restricted reverse profile and deep spike diving;
6. restricted multiday activity;
7. smooth coalescence of bounce and saturation limit points;
8. consistent diving protocols for altitude;
9. deep stops for decompression, extended range, and mixed gas diving with overall shorter decompression times, particularly for the shallow zone;
10. use of helium-rich mixtures for technical diving, with shallower isobaric switches to nitrox than suggested by Haldane strategies;
11. use of pure oxygen in the shallow zone to eliminate both dissolved and bubble inert gases.

Bubble models tend to be consistent with the utilitarian measures detailed above, and have the right signatures for diving applications across the full spectrum of activities. Or, said another way, bubble models are more powerful, more correct, and more inclusive. In terms of RGBM implementations, the mechanistics of dissolved gas buildup and elimination, inert gas diffusion across bubble interfaces, bubble excitation and elimination persistence time scales of minutes to hours from tissue friction, lipid and aqueous surfactant material properties, and Boyle expansion and contraction under ambient pressure change, are sufficient to address all of the above considerations.

So Mares, Zeagle, Plexus, Suunto, HydroSpace, and Abysmal Diving developed and released products (or are developing and releasing products) incorporating one such validated phase algorithm, the Reduced Gradient Bubble Model (RGBM), for diving. An iterative approach to staging diver ascents, the RGBM employs separated phase volumes as limit points, instead of the usual Haldane (maximum) critical tensions across tissue compartments. The model is tested and inclusive (altitude, repetitive, mixed gas, decompression, saturation, nonstop exposures), treating both dissolved and free gas phase buildup and elimination. NAUI Technical Diving employs the RGBM to schedule nonstop and decompression training protocols on trimix, helitrox, air, and nitrox, and will be releasing an exhaustive set of RGBM tables for those mixes shortly (some 500 pages of Tables). Included are constant oxygen partial pressure Tables for rebreathers. Mares, Dacor, and Plexus are also developing RGBM meters.

Suunto VYTEC/COBRA/STINGER are RGBM meters for recreational diving (plus nitrox), while ABYSS/RGBM is a licensed Abysmal Diving software product. The HydroSpace EXPLORER is a mixed gas decompression meter for technical and recreational diving, as is the ABYSS/RGBM software vehicle. All are first-time-ever commercial products with realistic implementation of a diving phase algorithm across a wide spectrum of exposure extremes. And all accommodate user knobs for aggressive to conservative diving. Expect RGBM algorithms to surface in other meters and software packages on the Internet. GAP is building a Palm Pilot with RGBM. NAUI Worldwide just released a set of no-group, no-calc, no-fuss recreational RGBM Tables for air and nitrox, sea level to 10,000 feet elevation.

The Countermeasures Dive Team at LANL employs the RGBM (last eight years). Military, commercial, and scientific sectors are using and further testing the RGBM. And scores of technical divers are reporting their RGBM profiles over the Internet and in technical diving publications. There are presently other major RGBM implementation projects in the works for meters and software packages.

The RGBM extends earlier work of the Tiny Bubble Group at the University of Hawaii, updating missing physics and extending their varying permeability model (VPM) to multidiving, altitude, and mixed gas applications. While certainly fundamental, the RGBM is also different and new on the diving scene. And not unexpectedly, the RGBM recovers the Haldane approach to decompression modeling in the limit of relatively safe (tolerably little) separated phase, with "tolerably little" a qualitative statement here. There is quite a bit more and different about the RGBM than other and related phase models. Differences focalize, in a word or two, on source generation mechanisms and persistence time scales for bubbles and seeds, bubble structural mechanics and materials, consistent treatment of all bubble expansion and contraction venues, and real world testing.

RGBM UNDERPINNINGS

Here, intent is to just look at the underpinnings of table, meter, and diveware implementations of the RGBM algorithm, one with extended range of applicability based on simple dual phase principles. Haldane approaches have dominated decompression algorithms for a very long time, and the RGBM has been long in coming on the commercial scene. With technical diving interest in deep stop modeling, helium, and concerns with repetitive diving in the recreational and technical community, phase modeling is timely and pertinent.

The establishment and evolution of gas phases involve overlapping steps:

1. nucleation and stabilization (free phase inception);
2. supersaturation (dissolved gas buildup);
3. excitation and growth (free-dissolved phase interaction);
4. coalescence (bubble aggregation);
5. deformation and occlusion (tissue damage and ischemia).

The computational issues of bubble dynamics (formation, growth, and elimination) are mostly outside Haldane framework, but get folded into halftime specifications in a nontractable mode. The very slow tissue compartments (halftimes large, or diffusivities small) might be tracking both free and dissolved gas exchange in poorly perfused regions. Free and dissolved phases, however, do not behave the same way under decompression. Care must be exercised in applying model equations to each component. In the presence of increasing proportions of free phases, dissolved gas equations cannot track either species accurately. Computational algorithms tracking both dissolved and free phases offer broader perspectives and expeditious alternatives, but with some changes from classical schemes. Free and dissolved gas dynamics differ. The driving force (gradient) for free phase elimination increases with depth, directly opposite to the dissolved phase elimination gradient which decreases with depth. Then, changes in operational procedures become necessary for optimality. Considerations of excitation and growth invariably require deeper staging procedures than supersaturation methods. Not as dramatic, similar constraints remain operative in multiexposures.

Other issues concerning time sequencing of symptoms impact computational algorithms. That bubble formation is a predisposing condition for decompression sickness is universally accepted. However, formation mechanisms and their ultimate physiological effect are two related, yet distinct, issues. On this point, most hypotheses make little distinction between bubble formation and the onset of bends symptoms. Yet we know that silent bubbles have been detected in subjects not suffering from decompression sickness. So it would thus appear that bubble formation, per se, and bends symptoms do not map onto each other in a one-to-one manner. Other factors are truly operative, such as the amount of gas dumped from solution, the size of nucleation sites receiving the gas, permissible bubble growth rates, deformation of surrounding tissue medium, and coalescence mechanisms for small bubbles into large aggregates, to name a few. These issues are the pervue of bubble theories, but the complexity of mechanisms addressed does not lend itself easily to table, nor even meter, implementation. But implement and improve we must, so consider the RGBM issues and tacks taken in the Suunto, Mares, Zeagle, HydroSpace, GAP, and ABYSS implementations.

INERT AND METABOLIC GAS TRANSPORT

Perfusion and diffusion are two mechanisms by which inert and metabolic gases exchange between tissue and blood. Perfusion denotes the blood flow rate in simplest terms, while diffusion refers to the gas penetration rate in tissue, or across tissue-blood boundaries. Each mechanism has a characteristic rate constant for the process. The smallest rate constant limits the gas exchange process. When diffusion rate constants are smaller than perfusion rate constants, diffusion dominates the tissue-blood gas exchange process, and vice versa. In the body, both processes play a role in real exchange process, especially considering the diversity of tissues and their geometries. The tissue halftimes are the inverses of perfusion rates, while the diffusivity of water scores the diffusion rate.

Inert gas transfer and coupled bubble growth are influenced by metabolic oxygen consumption. Consumption of oxygen and production of carbon dioxide drops the tissue oxygen tension below its level in the lungs, while carbon dioxide tension rises only slightly because carbon dioxide is 25 times more soluble than oxygen. Figure 1 compares partial pressures of oxygen, nitrogen, water vapor, and carbon dioxide in dry air, alveolar air, arterial blood, venous blood, and tissue.

FIGURE 1 - INHERENT UNSATURATION

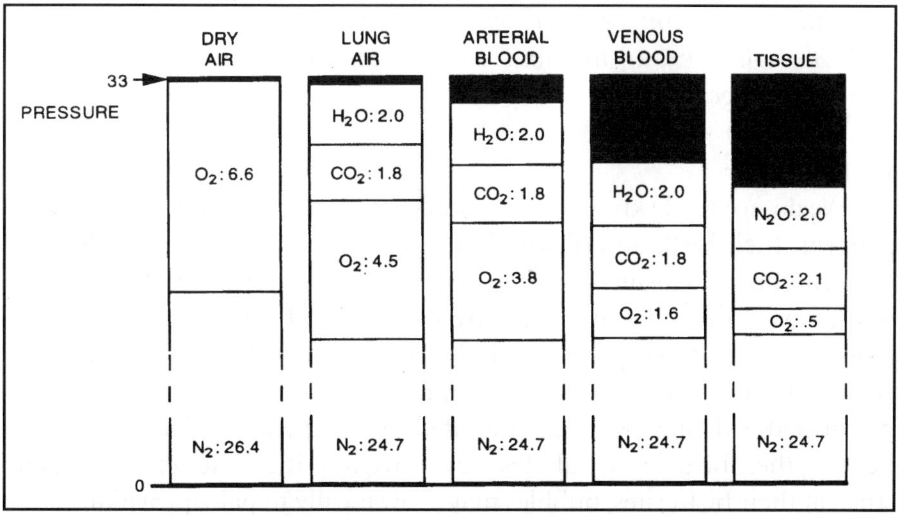

	DRY AIR	LUNG AIR	ARTERIAL BLOOD	VENOUS BLOOD	TISSUE
PRESSURE 33 →		H_2O: 2.0	H_2O: 2.0		
	O_2: 6.6	CO_2: 1.8	CO_2: 1.8	H_2O: 2.0	H_2O: 2.0
		O_2: 4.5	O_2: 3.8	CO_2: 1.8	CO_2: 2.1
				O_2: 1.6	O_2: .5
0	N_2: 26.4	N_2: 24.7	N_2: 24.7	N_2: 24.7	N_2: 24.7

Arterial and venous blood, and tissue, are clearly unsaturated with respect to dry air at 1 *atm*. Water vapor content is constant, and carbon dioxide variations are slight, though sufficient to establish an outgradient between tissue and blood. Oxygen tensions in tissue and blood are considerably below lung oxygen partial pressure, establishing the necessary ingradient for oxygenation and metabolism. Experiments also suggest that the degree of unsaturation increases linearly with pressure for constant composition breathing mixture, and decreases linearly with mole fraction of inert gas in the inspired mix.

Since tissues are unsaturated with respect to ambient pressure, one might exploit this window in bringing divers to the surface. By scheduling the ascent strategically, so that nitrogen (or any other inert breathing gas) supersaturation just takes up this unsaturation, total tissue tension can be kept at ambient pressure, an approach called the zero supersaturation ascent.

The RGBM treats coupled perfusion-diffusion transport as a two-step flow process, with blood flow (perfusion) serving as a boundary condition for tissue gas penetration (diffusion). Depending on time scales and rate coefficients, one or another (or both) processes dominate the exchange. However, for the Suunto, Mares, Zeagle, Hydrospace, Plexus, GAP, and ABYSS implementations, perfusion is assumed to dominate, simplifying matters and permitting online calculations. Additionally, tissues and blood are naturally undersaturated with respect to ambient pressure at equilibration through the mechanism of biological inherent unsaturation (oxygen window), and the RGBM includes this debt in calculations. Independent of perfusion- or diffusion-dominated gas transport, the RGBM tracks bubble excitation and number, inert gas transfer across the surfactant skin, and Boyle-like expansion and contraction of bubbles with ambient pressure changes.

BUBBLES

We do not really know where bubbles form nor lodge, their migration patterns, their birth and dissolution mechanisms, nor the exact chain of physico-chemical insults resulting in decompression sickness. Many possibilities exist, differing in the nature of the insult, the location, and the manifestation of symptoms. Bubbles might form directly (*de novo*) in supersaturated sites upon decompression, or possibly grow from preformed, existing seed nuclei excited by compression-decompression. Leaving their birth sites, bubbles may move to critical sites elsewhere. Or, stuck at their birth sites, bubbles may grow locally to pain-provoking size.

They might dissolve locally by gaseous diffusion to surrounding tissue or blood, or passing through screening filters, such as the lung complex, they might be broken down into smaller aggregates, or eliminated completely. Whatever the bubble history, it presently escapes complete elucidation. But whatever the process, the end result is very simple; both separated and dissolved gas must be treated in the transfer process.

Bubbles may hypothetically form in the blood (intravascular) or outside the blood (extravascular). Once formed, intravascularly or extravascularly, a number of critical insults are possible. Intravascular bubbles may stop in closed circulatory vessels and induce ischemia, blood sludging, chemistry degradations, or mechanical nerve deformation. Circulating gas emboli may occlude the arterial flow, clog the pulmonary filters, or leave the circulation to lodge in tissue sites as extravasular bubbles. Extravascular bubbles may remain locally in tissue sites, assimilating gas by diffusion from adjacent supersaturated tissue and growing until a nerve ending is deformed beyond its pain threshold. Or, extravascular bubbles might enter the arterial or venous flows, at which point they become intravascular bubbles.

To satisfy thermodynamic laws, bubbles assume spherical shapes in the absence of external or mechanical (distortion) pressures. Bubbles entrain free gases because of a thin film, exerting surface tension pressure on the gas. Hydrostatic pressure balance requires that the pressure inside the bubble exceed ambient pressure by the amount of surface tension, γ. Figure 2 depicts the pressure balance in a spherical (air) bubble. At small radii, surface tension pressure is greatest, and at large radii, surface tension pressure is least.

Gases will also diffuse into or out of a bubble according to differences in gas partial pressures inside and outside the bubble, whether in free or dissolved phases outside the bubble. In the former case, the gradient is termed free-free, while in the latter case, the gradient is termed free-dissolved. Unless the surface tension is identically zero, there is always a gradient tending to force gas out of the bubble, thus making the bubble collapse on itself because of surface tension pressure. If surrounding external pressures on bubbles change in time, however, bubbles may grow or contract. Figure 3 sketches bubble gas diffusion under instantaneous hydrostatic equilibrium for an air bubble.

Bubbles grow or contract according to the strength of the free-free or free-dissolved gradient, and it is the latter case which concerns divers under decompression. The radial rate at which bubbles grow or contract

FIGURE 2 - BUBBLE PRESSURE BALANCE

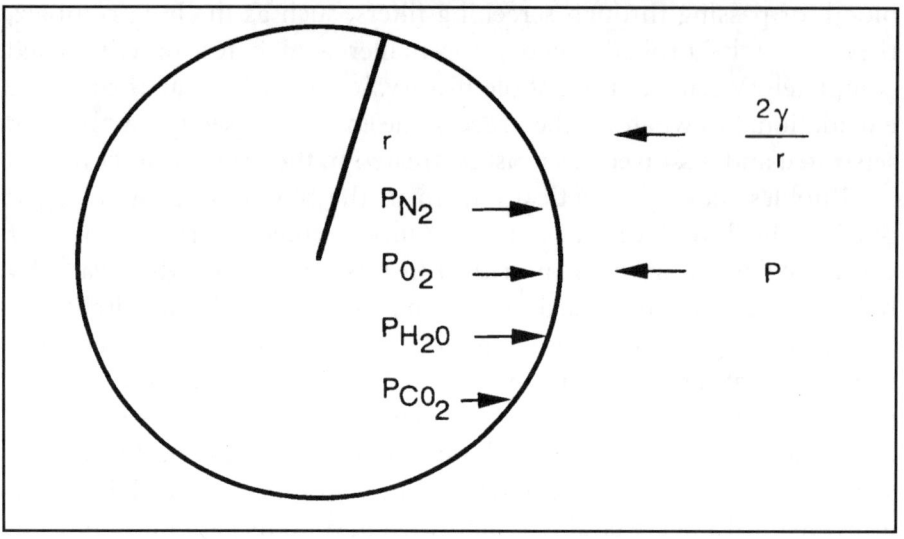

FIGURE 3 - BUBBLE GAS DIFFUSION

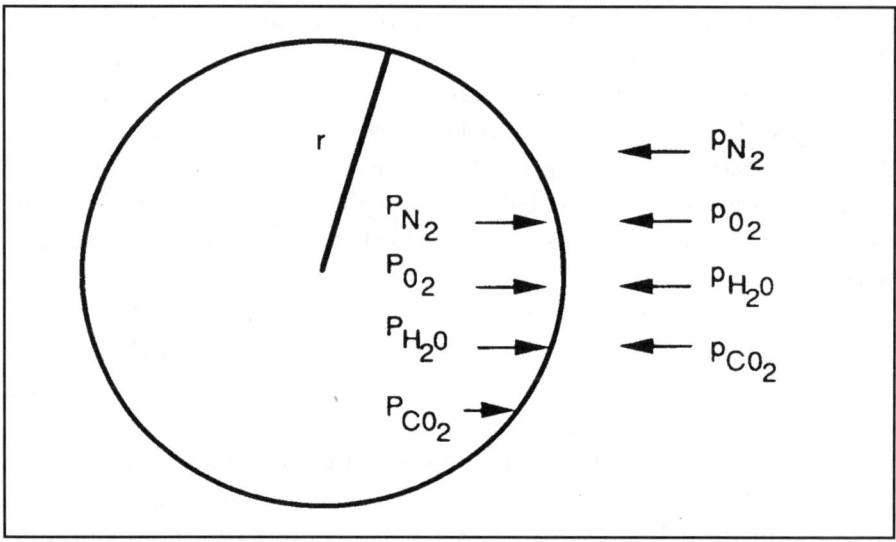

depends directly on the diffusivity and solubility, and inversely on the bubble radius. A critical (excitation) radius, ε, separates growing from contracting bubbles. Bubbles with radius $r > \varepsilon$ will grow, while bubbles with radius $r < \varepsilon$ will contract. Limiting bubble growth and adverse impact upon nerves and circulation are issues when decompressing divers and aviators.

Bubbles grow or contract by gaseous diffusion across the thin film interface, due to dissolved gas gradients. Bubbles also expand or contract upon pressure changes according to Boyle-like equations of state (EOS), with the expansion or contraction rate a function of the material composition of the surfactants coating the inside of the bubble. Material behavior can vary from thin elastic films to almost solid shell beebees, depending on coefficients and pressure regimes of EOS.

The RGBM assumes that a size distribution of seeds (potential bubbles) is always present, and that a certain number is excited into growth by compression-decompression. An iterative process for ascent staging is employed to control the inflation rate of these growing bubbles so that their collective volume never exceeds a phase volume limit point. Gas mixtures of helium, nitrogen, and oxygen contain bubble distributions of different sizes, but possess the same phase volume limit point. Distributions have lifetimes of minutes to many hours, impacting repetitive, reverse profile, multiday, altitude, and gas mixes on varying time scales. Colloidal particles are not the stabilizing material inside seeds and bubbles.

Temperature

Bubbles are affected by temperature much like gases, but only coupled through skin EOS of the material surrounding the gases inside the bubbles. Broadly speaking, bubbles will expand with temperature increases, and contract with temperature decreases, all subject to skin behavior, and material properties of same.

The effects of temperature over nominal water temperatures and diving activities are small, especially since body core temperatures and those of surrounding tissues and blood vary little under changes in outside temperature. Some data support higher DCS incidence rates for divers undergoing both warm-to-cold and cold-to-warm temperature switches following diving. But more reliable data support higher DCS incidence in warm environments versus colder ones. Naval Special Warfare suggests that underwater operations in temperature zones above 90°F pose higher risks to SEALs. Divers salvaging TWA 200 in hot suits exhibited a higher proportion of DCS than those in wet suits. Back in the early '50s, USN studies suggested that divers in colder waters (45°C) had lower DCS incidence rates than divers in warmer waters (73°C).

Still, cold divers are expected to eliminate inert gases slower than warm divers, and so risk of DCS might increase in divers who are cold following exposure. Doppler studies by Dunford and Hayward in the early '80s confirm the presence of more VGE in warm divers versus cold divers. Of course, if DCS correlates with Doppler score, these warm divers should be at higher risk. And they were not.

The RGBM treats temperature explicitly in skin EOS and staging regimens. Warmer temperatures promote larger bubbles and bubble seeds. Colder temperatures, however, in warm-to-cold temperature switches also provide a fracture mechanism for skins through the EOS. The fracture mechanics suggest a means to bubble depletion in the model.

Bubble Seeds

Bubbles, which are unstable, are thought to grow from micron size, gas nuclei which resist collapse due to elastic skins of surface activated molecules (surfactants), or possibly reduction in surface tension at tissue interfaces or crevices. If families of these micronuclei persist, they vary in size and surfactant content. Large pressures (not really known) are necessary to crush them. Micronuclei are small enough to pass through the pulmonary filters, yet dense enough not to float to the surfaces of their environments, with which they are in both hydrostatic (pressure) and diffusion (gas flow) equilibrium. When nuclei are stabilized, and not activated to growth or contraction by external pressure changes, the skin (surfactant) tension offsets both the Laplacian (film) tension and any mechanical help from surrounding tissue. Then all pressures and gas tensions are equal. However, on decompression, the seed pockets are surrounded by dissolved gases at high tension and can subsequently grow (bubbles) as surrounding gas diffuses into them. The rate at which bubbles grow, or contract, depends directly on the difference between tissue tension and local ambient pressure, effectively the bubble pressure gradient. At some point in time, a critical volume of bubbles, or separated gas, is established and bends symptoms become statistically more probable. On compression, the micronuclei are crunched down to smaller sizes across families, apparently stabilizing at new reduced size. Bubbles are also crunched by increasing pressure because of Boyle's law, and then additionally shrink if gas diffuses out of them. As bubbles get smaller and smaller, they probably restabilize as micronuclei.

The RGBM postulates bubble seeds with lipid or aqueous surfactants. Bubble skins are assumed permeable under all ambient pressure, unlike the VPM. The size of seeds excited into growth is inversely proportional to the supersaturation gradient. RGBM excitation radii, ε, start in the 0.01 μm range, far smaller than other dual phase models, because the RGBM tracks Boyle expansion and bubble gas diffusion across the tissue seed interface *(across the surfactant). At increasing pressure, bubble seeds permit gas diffusion at a slower rate. The RGBM assumes bubble skins are stabilized by surfactants over calculable time scales, producing seeds that are variably persistent in the body. Bubble skins are probably molecularly activated, complex biosubstances found throughout the body. Whatever the formation process, the RGBM assumes the size distribution is exponentially decreasing in size, that is, more smaller seeds than larger seeds in exponential proportions. Skin response of the bubbles to pressure change is dictated by a material equation-of-state (EOS), again unlike others. As stated, the RGBM diffuses gas from tissues to bubbles (and vice versa) using a transfer equation across the film interface. This requires a mass transfer coefficient dependent on the gas solubility and diffusivity. The source of bubbles and seeds is probably tribonucleation due to muscle and tissue interfriction, and persistence time scales range from minutes to many hours, according to Powell.*

SLOW TISSUE COMPARTMENTS

Based on concerns in multiday and heavy repetitive diving, with the hope of controlling staircasing gas buildup in exposures through critical tensions, slow tissue compartments (halftimes greater than 80 minutes) have been incorporated into some algorithms. Calculations, however, show that virtually impossible exposures are required of the diver before critical tensions are even approached, literally tens of hours of near continuous activity. As noted in many calculations, slow compartment cannot really control multidiving through critical tensions, unless critical tensions are reduced to absurd levels, inconsistent with nonstop time limits for shallow exposures. That is a model limitation, not necessarily a physical reality. The physical reality is that bubbles in slow tissues are eliminated over time scales of days, and the model limitation is that the arbitrary parameter space does not accommodate such phenomena.

And that is no surprise either, when one considers that dissolved gas models are not supposed to track bubbles and free phases. Repetitive exposures do provide fresh dissolved gas for excited nuclei and growing free phases, but it is not the dissolved gas which is the problem just by itself. When bubble growth is considered, the slow compartments appear very important, because, therein, growing free phases are mostly left undisturbed insofar as surrounding tissue tensions are concerned. Bubbles grow more gradually in slow compartments because the gradient there is typically small, yet grow over longer time scales. When coupled to free phase dynamics, slow compartments are necessary in multidiving calculations.

The RGBM incorporates a spectrum of tissue compartments, ranging from 1 min to 480 min depending on gas mixture (helium, nitrogen, oxygen). Phase separation and bubble growth in slower compartments is a central focus in calculations over long time scales, and the same for fast tissue compartments over short time scales, that is, scales over 2 or 3 times the compartment halftime.

VENOUS GAS EMBOLI

While the numbers of venous gas emboli (VGE) detected with ultrasound Doppler techniques can be correlated with nonstop limits, and the limits then used to fine-tune the critical tension matrix for select exposure ranges, fundamental issues are not necessarily resolved by venous gas emboli measurements. First of all, venous gas emboli are probably not the direct cause of bends per se, unless they block the pulmonary circulation, or pass through the pulmonary traps and enter the arterial system to lodge in critical sites. Intravascular bubbles might first form at extravascular sites. According to studies, electron micrographs have highlighted bubbles breaking into capillary walls from adjacent lipid tissue beds in mice. Fatty tissue, draining the veins and possessing few nerve endings, is thought to be an extravascular site of venous gas emboli. Similarly, since blood constitutes no more than 8% of the total body capacity for dissolved gas, the bulk of circulating blood does not account for the amount of gas detected as venous gas emboli. Secondly, what has not been established is the link between venous gas emboli, possible micronuclei, and bubbles in critical tissues. Any such correlations of venous gas emboli with tissue micronuclei would unquestionably require considerable first-hand knowledge of nuclei size distributions, sites, and tissue thermodynamic properties. While some believe that venous gas emboli correlate with bubbles in extravascular sites, such as tendons and ligaments, and that venous gas emboli measurements can be reliably applied to bounce diving, the correlations with repetitive and saturation diving have not been made to work, nor important correlations with more severe forms of decompression sickness, such as chokes and central nervous system (CNS) hits.

Still, whatever the origin of venous gas emboli, procedures and protocols which reduce gas phases in the venous circulation deserve attention, for that matter, anywhere else in the body. The moving Doppler bubble may not be the bends bubble, but perhaps the difference may only be the present site. The propensity of venous gas emboli may reflect the state of critical tissues where decompression sickness does occur. Studies and tests based on Doppler detection of venous gas emboli are still the only viable means of monitoring free phases in the body.

The RGBM uses nonstop time limits tuned to recent Doppler measurements, conservatively reducing them along the lines originally suggested by Spencer (and others), but within the phase volume constraint. The Mares, Dacor, and Suunto implementations penalize ascent violations by requiring additional safety stop time dictated by risk analysis of the violation. All RGBM implementations supply user knobs for aggressive to conservative diving modifications, thru EOS in the full versions and M-values in the Haldane folded algorithms. Doppler scores over surface intervals are employed to calibrate RGBM bubble factors, both short and long intervals.

Multidiving

Concerns with multidiving can be addressed through variable critical gradients, then tissue tensions in Haldane models. While variable gradients or tensions are difficult to codify in table frameworks, they are easy to implement in digital meters. Reductions in critical parameters also result from the phase volume constraint, a constraint employing the separated volume of gas in tissue as trigger point for the bends, not dissolved gas buildup alone in tissue compartments. In the VPM the phase volume is proportional to the product of the dissolved-free gas gradient times a bubble number representing the number of gas nuclei excited into growth by the compression-decompression, replacing just slow tissue compartments in controlling multidiving. In the RGBM, the phase volume depends on the number of seeds excited and the Boyle and gas diffusion expansion-contraction of the seeds excited into growth.

In considering bubbles and free-dissolved gradients within critical phase hypotheses, repetitive criteria develop which require reductions in Haldane critical tensions or dissolved-free gas gradients. This reduction simply arises from lessened degree of bubble elimination over repetitive intervals, compared to long bounce intervals, and need to reduce bubble inflation rate through smaller driving gradients. Deep repetitive and spike exposures feel the greatest effects of gradient reduction, but shallower multiday activities are impacted. Bounce diving enjoys long surface intervals to eliminate bubbles while repetitive diving must contend with shorter intervals, and hypothetically reduced time for bubble elimination. Theoretically, a reduction in the bubble inflation driving term, namely, the tissue gradient or tension, holds the inflation rate down. Overall, concern is bubble excess driven by dissolved gas. And then both bubbles and dissolved gas are important. In such an approach, multidiving exposures experience reduced permissible tensions through lessened free phase elimination over time spans of two days. Parameters are consistent with bubble experiments, and both slow and fast tissue compartments must be considered.

The RGBM reduces the phase volume limit in multidiving by considering free phase elimination and buildup during surface intervals, depending on altitude, time, and depth of previous profiles. Repetitive, multiday, and reverse profile exposures are tracked and impacted by critical phase volume reductions over appropriate time scales.

ADAPTATION

Divers and caisson workers have long contended that tolerance to decompression sickness increases with daily diving, and decreases after a few weeks layoff, that in large groups of compressed air workers, new workers were at higher risk than those who were exposed to high pressure regularly. This acclimatization might result from either increased body tolerance to bubbles (physiological adaptation), or decreased number and volume of bubbles (physical adaptation). Test results are totally consistent with physical adaptation.

Yet, there is slight inconsistency here. Statistics point to slightly higher bends incidence in repetitive and multiday diving. Some hyperbaric specialists confirm the same, based on experience. The situation is not clear, but the resolution plausibly links to the kinds of first dives made and repetitive frequency in the sequence. If the first in a series of repetitive dives are kept short, deep, and conservative with respect to nonstop time limits, initial excitation and growth are minimized. Subsequent dives would witness minimal levels of initial phases. If surface intervals are also long enough to optimize both free and dissolved gas elimination, any nuclei excited into growth could be efficiently eliminated outside repetitive exposures, with adaptation occurring over day intervals as noted in experiments. But higher frequency, repetitive and multiday loading may not afford sufficient surface intervals to eliminate free phases excited by earlier exposures, with additional nuclei then possibly excited on top of existing phases. Physical adaptation seems less likely, and decompression sickness more likely, in the latter case. Daily regimens of a single bounce dive with slightly increasing exposure times are consistent with physical adaptation, and conservative practices.

The regimens also require deepest dives first. In short, acclimatization is as much a question of eliminating any free phases formed as it is a question of crushing or reducing nuclei as potential bubbles in repetitive exposures. And then time scales on the order of a day might limit the adaptation process.

The RGBM generates bubble seed distributions on time scales of minutes for fast tissues and hours for slow tissues, adding new bubbles to existing bubbles in calculations. Phase volume limit points are also reduced by the added effects of new bubbles. Repetitive and reverse profile diving are impacted by bubble growth in the fast compartments, while flying after diving and multiday diving are affected by bubble growth in the slow compartments.

Crucial to all modern decompression models is the concept of limiting separated phase, or phase volume, as opposed to (just) limiting tensions in various arbitrary tissue compartments. This phase volume depends on numbers of bubbles excited into growth, gas diffusion into the bubbles, and Boyle expansion-contraction of the gas assembly under pressure changes. And that is the focus of the mathematical reduced gradient bubble model, coming up after first detailing some material dynamics pertinent to the RGBM.

• MATERIAL DYNAMICS •

Bubbles and seeds in the body probably contain countless biosubstances which defy material representation, do not form and deform as simple gas bubbles, and possess variable persistence time scales depending on position in the body, external and internal pressures, and surrounding blood and tissue. However complex, we can still get a rough handle on their response by assigning some coarse material properties.

SURFACE TENSION

Discontinuities in types of materials and/or densities at surfaces and interfaces give rise to interfacial forces, called *surface tension*. Discontinuities in density produce cohesive gradients tending to diminish density at the surface region. At the interfaces between immiscible materials, cohesive forces produce surface tension, but adhesional forces between dissimilar materials tend to offset (decrease) the interfacial tension. Surface and interfacial tension are readily observed in fluids, but less readily in solids. In solids, very little stretching of the surface region can occur if the solids are rigid. Upon heating rigid solids to higher temperature, surface tension becomes a discernible effect.

Any two phases in equilibrium are separated by a surface of contact, the existence of which also produces surface tension. The thin contact region is a transition layer, sometimes called the *film* layer. Phases can be solid, liquid, or vapor, with surface tension in each case different. The actual position, or displacement, of the phase boundary may alter the area of the phases on either side, leading to pressure differences in the phases. The difference between phase pressures is known as the surface, or film, pressure. The phase equilibration condition requires the temperatures and chemical potentials (Gibbs free energy) of phases to be equal, but certainly not the pressures.

A simple description of measurable surface tension, γ, is linked to the magnitude of cohesive forces in materials a and b, denoted, χ_a and χ_b, wanting to pull the surfaces together, and the adhesional forces, α_a and α_b, wanting to draw the surfaces apart. The net surface tension, γ, is the sum of cohesive forces minus adhesive forces, that is,

$$\gamma = \chi_a + \chi_b - \alpha_a - \alpha_b.$$

Thermodynamically, surface tension contributes a differential work term, $d\omega$, to system balance equations given in terms of surface contact area, dA,

$$d\omega = \gamma \, dA$$

Surface tension pressure, τ, is surface tension force per unit area, that is, in terms of work function, ω,

$$\tau = -\left[\frac{\partial \omega}{\partial V}\right]_{S,T}$$

at constant entropy, S, and temperature, T. Interfacial tension in liquids is measured by the pressure difference across surfaces, again denoted a and b,

$$\tau = \gamma \left[\frac{1}{r_a} + \frac{1}{r_b}\right]$$

given radii of curvature, r_a and r_b. For thin films, such as bubbles, $r_a \approx r_b = r$, and we see,

$$\tau_{bub} = \frac{2\gamma}{r}$$

deduced by Young and Laplace almost two centuries past. For water, $\gamma = 50$ *dyne cm*, while for watery tissue, $\gamma = 18$ *dyne cm*, at STP, but we know surface tension is more generally a function of pressure and temperature for materials coating bubbles.

The surface of all solids and liquids adsorb foreign molecules from their surroundings. These adsorbed molecules change most of the chemical and physical properties of the underlying substrate. Adhesion, catalysis, corrosion, fracture, lubrication, and wear are affected by the topmost molecular layers on a surface. Understanding these changes involves close study of films themselves, as described. The forces of attraction that cause adsorption are relatively weak and are the long range interactions existing between all atoms and molecules.

Surfactants

Water, gasoline, glycerin, and salad oil are clearly liquids. Pancake syrup, plaster, eggwhite, silly putty, paint, glue, and soap are also liquids, that is, they flow on the application of stress, but border on classification otherwise. In mechanical response, the latter class differs from each other as much as they differ from solids. And the response is variable in time. Syrup becomes sticky as it dries. Dishwashing soap often dries into light flakes. Silly putty flows on tilt, but shatters on sudden impact. Airplane glue is springy and rubbery.

Substances in the latter category are called structured fluids, owing their distinctive and unusual properties to large polyatomic composites, many times the size of a water molecule. Fluids containing polyatomic structures manifest a wide variety of mechanical response and self organization. Body tissues and fluids host an uncountable variety of organic and inorganic matter, with many biochemical substances falling into structured fluid category. Among the structured fluids, a class of self assemblies, called surfactants, are very interesting, possessing properties which can stabilize microbubbles in various stages of evolution by offsetting surface tension.

A surfactant is a structured fluid which is *ambiphillic*, incorporating parts that assume preferential orientations at water-oil (immisicible) interfaces. A surfactant molecule usually consists of a bulky ion at one end, and a counter ion at the other. Isolated molecules cannot usually exist in one media type, or the other, but instead orient themselves into *micelles*, configurations in which like parts clump together, that is head in one substance and tail in the other. Micelles typically possess diameters near 10^{-3} μm, and render the interfaces unlike anything measured in the components. Lipid-aqueous tissue interfaces potentially present favorable environments for surfactants.

Under certain conditions, a surfactant can reduce interfacial surface tension, allowing the interface to grow and wrap around itself. The result is a microbundle full of alternating surfaces and interfaces, spherical in structure to minimize thermodynamic energy constraints. Many substances may be bound up in the microbundle. If small gas nuclei, but typically much larger than a micelle, are in contact with the interfaces, or surfactants directly, a spherical gas micronucleus-microemulsion can develop, varying in size and surfactant content. The assembly is stable when the effective surface tension is zero, when surfactant skin pressure just balances mechanical (Laplace) surface tension. If the effective surface tension of the microbubble, γ, is not zero, the collection will grow or contract until stable, or disassemble. In the case of gas microemulsions, the surfactant is thought to coat the inside boundary layer mostly, with free gas in the interior. The actual picture is probably more complex, but such a picture can be drawn for computational simplicity. Surfactant stabilized micronuclei may theoretically destabilize under compression-decompression processes in diving, perhaps spawning bubble growth fueled by high gas tension in surrounding media. Microbubbles may remain at the interfaces, but probably migrate. Sources of initial gas nuclei, surfactant composition, and tissue sites await description.

COMPRESSIBILITY AND CUBICAL EXPANSION

Under pressure and temperature changes, all matter undergoes expansion or compression. The coefficient of volume change, κ, under pressure change, at constant temperature, T, is called the *isothermal compressibility*,

$$\kappa = -\frac{1}{V}\left[\frac{\partial V}{\partial P}\right]_T$$

and the coefficient of cubical expansion, β, measures the volume change under temperature change, at constant pressure,

$$\beta = \frac{1}{V}\left[\frac{\partial V}{\partial T}\right]_P$$

and these quantities can certainly be measured experimentally for any material. The corresponding thermal coefficient, ζ, measures change of pressure, P, with temperature, T, at constant volume, V, and is simply related to κ and β through,

$$\zeta = \left[\frac{\partial P}{\partial T}\right]_V = -\left[\frac{\partial V}{\partial T}\right]_P \left[\frac{\partial V}{\partial P}\right]_T^{-1} = \frac{\beta}{\kappa}$$

For solids and liquids, β, κ, and ζ are very small, virtually constant over small ranges of temperature and pressure. For gases, the situation is different. Ideal gases, from the equation of state, simply have,

$$\kappa = \frac{1}{P}$$

$$\beta = \frac{1}{T}$$

so that compressibility and expansion coefficients depend inversely on pressure, P, and temperature, T. The thermal coefficient is similarly given by,

$$\zeta = \frac{P}{T} = \frac{nR}{v}$$

Bubble Metrics

During rapid compression from initial ambient pressure, P_i, to increased pressure, P, seeds and micronuclei are subject to crushing compression which decreases radial size. This produces increased tolerance to supersaturation in blood and tissues since smaller nuclei form macroscopic (unstable) bubbles less readily than larger ones. The greater the crushing pressure, $\Delta P = P - P_i$, the greater the supersaturation required to excite a given number of bubbles in the body. A given distribution of nuclei in the body has, for each ΔP, a critical (excitation) radius, r_i. Nuclei with radii less than r_i will not grow into bubbles, while nuclei with radii greater than r_i will be excited into growth. Said another way, all nuclei larger than r_i for any compression-decompression schedule, ΔP, will evolve into macroscopic bubbles while the rest will not. But just how excited micronuclei grow requires a model for the behavior of effective surface tension under compression-decompression, as described earlier. The model can be based on an equation-of-state

(EOS), or tied to data fits of *observed* bubble behavior in appropriate media. And the model does not necessarily depend upon the actual number distribution of seeds as a function of size (radius), though an exponential distribution is usually employed or inferred. On most counts in nature, seed distributions assume exponential forms.

Certainly we do not know the exact physical properties of gas seeds and bubbles in the body, but we can make some general comments based on known equation of state relationships. Phenomenological relationships fitted from laboratory experiments are also of interest.

Seed Material Response

Under changes in ambient pressure (and temperature), bubbles will grow or contract, both due to dissolved gas diffusion and Boyle's law. An *ideal* change under Boyle's law is symbolically written. Denoting initial and final pressures and volumes with subscripts, *i* and *f*, we have, with bubble volume,

$$P_i V_i = P_f V_f$$

for *r* the bubble radius. The above supposes totally flexible (almost ideal

$$V = \frac{4}{3}\pi r^3$$

gas) bubble films or skins on the inside, certainly not unrealistic for thin skin bubbles. Similarly, if the response to small incremental pressure changes of the bubble skins is a smooth and slowly varying function, the above is also true in low order. Obviously, the relationship reduces to,

$$P_i r_i^3 = P_f r_f^3$$

for an ideal radial response to pressure change.

But for real structured, molecular membranes, capable of offsetting constrictive surface tension, the response to Boyle's law is modified, and can be cast in terms of Boyle modifiers, ξ,

$$\xi_i P_i V_i = \xi_f P_f V_f$$

with ξ virial functions depending on *P*, *V*, and *T*. For thin and elastic bubble skins, $\xi = 1$. For all else, $\xi \neq 1$. For gels studied in the laboratory, as an instance, surfactant stabilized micronuclei do not behave like ideal gas seeds with thin elastic films. Instead under compression-decompression, their behavior is always less than ideal. That is to say, volume changes under compression or decompression are always less than computed by Boyle's law, similar to the response of a wet suit, sponge, tissue bed, or lung membrane. The growth or contraction of seeds according to an EOS is more complex than Boyle's law. The virial expansion has for all P, T, V and mole fractions, n, for R the universal gas constant,

$$PV = nRT \sum_{i=0}^{N} \alpha_i \left[\frac{nT}{V} \right]^i$$

or, treating the virial expansion as a Boyle modifier, ξ,

$$\xi PV = nRT$$

across data points and regions. Symbolically, the radius, r, can be cast,

$$r = \sum_{i=0}^{N} \beta_i \left[\frac{nRT}{P} \right]^{i/3}$$

or, again introducing Boyle modifiers, ζ,

$$\zeta r = \left[\frac{nRT}{P} \right]^{1/3}$$

for α and β standard virial constants. Obviously, the virial modifiers, ξ and ζ, are the inverses of the virial sum expansions as power series. For small deviations from thin film bubble structures, both are close to one.

Observationally, though, the parameterization can take a more limited tack. In gel experiments, the EOS is replaced by two regions, the permeable (simple gas diffusion across the bubble interface) and impermeable (rather restricted gas diffusion across the bubble interface). In the permeable region, seeds act like thin film bubbles for gas transfer. In the impermeable region, seeds might be likened to beebees. An EOS of course can recover this response in both limits.

Accordingly, just in gels, the corresponding change in critical radius, r, following compression, $(P - P_i)$, in the *permeable* region, satisfies a relationship, according to Yount,

$$(P - P_i) = 2(\gamma_c - \gamma) \left| \frac{1}{r} - \frac{1}{r_i} \right|$$

with γ_c maximum compressional strength of the surfactant skin, γ the surface tension, and r_i the critical radius at P_i. When P exceeds the structure breakpoint, P_c, an equation for the *impermeable* region must be used. For crushing pressure differential, $P - P_c$, the gel model requires,

$$P - P_c = 2(\gamma_c - \gamma)\left[\frac{1}{r} - \frac{1}{r_c}\right] + P_c + 2P_i + P_i\left[\frac{r_c}{r}\right]^3$$

where,

$$r_c = \left[\frac{P_c - P_i}{2(\gamma_c - \gamma)} + \frac{1}{r_i}\right]^{-1}$$

is the radius of the critical nucleus at the onset of impermeability, obtained by replacing P and r with P_c and r_c above. The allowed tissue supersaturation, $\Delta\Pi$, is given by,

$$\Delta\Pi = 2\frac{\gamma}{\gamma_c r}(\gamma_c - \gamma)$$

with, in the permeable region,

$$r = \left[\frac{P - P_i}{2(\gamma_c - \gamma)} + \frac{1}{r_i}\right]^{-1}$$

and, in the impermeable region,

$$r^3 - 2(\gamma_c - \gamma)r^2 - \frac{P_i}{\zeta}r_c^3 = 0$$

for,

$$\zeta = P - 2P_c + 2P_i + \frac{2(\gamma_c - \gamma)}{r_c}$$

Thus, allowed supersaturation is a function of three parameters, γ, γ_c, and r_i. They can be fitted to exposures and lab data. Boyle expansion or contraction needs be applied to the excited seeds. Additionally, gas diffuses into and out of bubbles under ambient pressure changes, so that material property needs specification for gas transfer.

With material dynamics finished, we turn to phase volume limits, the controlling critical parameters for dual phase models and the RGBM.

· CRITICAL PHASE VOLUME LIMIT ·

A complete approach to imposing phase volume limits, incorporating both gas diffusion across tissue-bubble interfaces and Boyle expansion-contraction, is used in the dual phase reduced gradient bubble model.

PHASE EXPOSURE INTEGRAL

The phase volume constraint equation is rewritten in terms of a phase function, ϕ, varying in time,

$$\int_0^\tau \frac{\partial \phi}{\partial t} \, dt \leq \Phi$$

with, simplifying notation,

$$\dot{\phi} = \frac{\partial \phi}{\partial t}$$

for Φ the separated phase, and τ some (long) cutoff time. Specifically, for Φ total gas tension, V bubble volume, D gas diffusivity, r bubble radius, n bubble number as a function of radius, γ bubble surface tension, P and T absolute pressure and temperature, we have,

$$\dot{\phi} = \left[\frac{\partial V}{\partial t}\right]_{diffusion} + \left[\frac{\partial V}{\partial t}\right]_{Boyle} + \left[\frac{\partial V}{\partial t}\right]_{excitation}$$

for,

$$\left[\frac{\partial V}{\partial t}\right]_{diffusion} = 4\pi DS \int_\varepsilon^\infty nr\left(\Pi - P - \frac{2\gamma}{r}\right) dr$$

$$\left[\frac{\partial V}{\partial t}\right]_{Boyle} = \int_\varepsilon^\infty n\left(\frac{T}{P}\frac{\partial}{\partial t}\frac{PV}{T}\right) dr$$

$$\left[\frac{\partial V}{\partial t}\right]_{excitation} = \frac{\partial}{\partial t}\left(4\pi \int_\varepsilon^\infty nr^2 dr\right)$$

and all other quantities as denoted previously, and the bubble number integrand normalized,

$$\int_0^\infty n \, dr = 1$$

The integrals over bubble radii sum up the collective phase of all seeds (larger than a critical radius depending on material properties) excited into growth. Note that all bubble seeds in the distribution are included in the treatement (above the critical radius, that is).

The temporal phase function, ϕ, depends on number of bubbles, n, stimulated into growth by compression-decompression, the supersaturation gradient, G, seed expansion-contraction by radial diffusion, $\partial r/\partial t$, Boyle expansion-contraction, PV, under pressure changes, and temperature, T, in general. The excitation radius, ε, depends on the material properties, and is deduced for air (μm), following Adamson, Fischer, Frenkel, and Hirschfelder,

$$\varepsilon = 0.00713 + 0.00158 \left[\frac{T}{P}\right]^{1/3} + 0.03262 \left[\frac{T}{P}\right]^{2/3}$$

with P given in fsw, and T measured in absolute K^o, and with ranges for virial coefficients, aqueous to lipid materials, varying by factors of 0.75 to 4.86 times the values listed above. Values of the excitation radii, ε, above range from 0.01 to 0.05 μm for sea level down to 500 fsw. This is compared to excitation radii in other models (varying permeability and tissue bubble diffusion models) which vary in the 1 μm range. For instance, in gel experiments, the excitation radius, r, is fitted to the form,

$$\frac{1}{r} = 1.30 + \frac{\Delta P}{2\gamma}$$

with 2γ a colloidal constant, suggested by data fits ($fsw\,\mu m$),

$$2\gamma = 135.3 \left[\frac{P}{T}\right]^{1/4} + 73.6 \left[\frac{P}{T}\right]^{1/2} - 15.9 \left[\frac{P}{T}\right]^{3/4}$$

for ΔP excitation pressure differential, and P final pressure. Radii in the gel expressions are 1 μm and smaller. RGBM values for pure helium and nitrogen are recounted later. And the air expression above represents a good RGBM fit to exposure data across lipid and aqueous representations.

REPETITIVE EXPOSURES

The phase integral for multiexposures is written, for any number of J dives, or dive segments,

$$\sum_{j=1}^{J} \left[\dot{\phi}\, t_{d_j} + \int_0^{t_j} \dot{\phi}\, dt\right] \leq \Phi$$

CRITICAL PHASE VOLUME LIMIT

with the index j denoting each dive segment, up to a total of J, and t_j the surface interval after the jth segment. For the inequality to hold, that is, for the sum of all growth rate terms to total less than Φ, obviously each term must be less the Φ. Assuming that $t_J \to \infty$, gives,

$$\sum_{j=1}^{J-1}\left[\dot\phi\left[t_{d_j} + \lambda^{-1} - \lambda^{-1}\exp(-\lambda t_j)\right]\right] + \dot\phi\left(t_{d_J} + \lambda^{-1}\right) \leq \Phi$$

Defining $\dot\phi_j$,

$$\dot\phi_j\left(t_{d_j} + \lambda^{-1}\right) = \dot\phi\left(t_{d_j} + \lambda^{-1}\right) - \dot\phi\lambda^{-1}\exp\left(-\lambda t_{j-1}\right)$$

for $j = 2$ to J, and,

$$\dot\phi_1 = \dot\phi$$

for $j=1$, it follows that

$$\sum_{j=1}^{J}\dot\phi_j\left(t_{d_j} + \lambda^{-1}\right) \leq \Phi$$

with the important property,

$$\dot\phi_j \leq \dot\phi.$$

This implies we employ reduced phase functions extracted from bounce phase functions by writing,

$$\dot\phi_j = \xi_j\dot\phi$$

with ξ_j a *multidiving* fraction requisitely satisfying,

$$0 \leq \xi_j \leq 1$$

so that, as needed,

$$\dot\phi_j \leq \dot\phi.$$

The fractions, ξ, applied to $\dot\phi$ always reduce them. As time and repetitive frequency increase, the body's ability to eliminate load bubbles and nuclei decreases, so that we restrict the permissible bubble load in time by writing,

$$\dot{\phi}(t_{j-1}^{cum}) = N\beta\varepsilon\left[1 - \frac{\varepsilon(t_{j-1}^{cum})}{\varepsilon}\right] = \dot{\phi}\exp\left(-\lambda_r t_{j-1}^{cum}\right)$$

$$t_{j-1}^{cum} = \sum_{i=1}^{j-1} t_i$$

with t_{j-1}^{cum} cumulative dive time. A reduction factor, η_j^{rg}, accounting for creation of new micronuclei is taken to be the ratio of present load over initial load, written,

$$\eta_j^{rg} = \frac{\dot{\phi}(t_{j-1}^{cum})}{\dot{\phi}} = \exp\left(-\lambda_r t_{j-1}^{cum}\right)$$

For reverse profile diving, the phase function is restricted by the ratio (minimum value) of the bubble load on the present segment to the bubble load at the deepest point over segments. The phase function reduction, η_j^{ex}, is then written,

$$\eta_j^{ex} = \frac{(\dot{\phi})_{max}}{(\dot{\phi})_j} = \frac{(\varepsilon P)_{max}}{(\varepsilon P)_j}$$

with εP the product of the appropriate excitation radius and pressure. Because bubble elimination periods are shortened over repetitive dives, compared to intervals for bounce dives, the phase function reduction, η_j^{rp}, is proportional to the difference between maximum and actual surface bubble growth rate, that is,

$$\eta_j^{rp} = 1 - \left[1 - \frac{\dot{\phi}_{min}}{\dot{\phi}}\right]\exp\left(-\lambda_m t_{j-1}\right)$$

with t_{j-1} consecutive total dive time, λ_m^{-1} on the order of an hour, and $\dot{\phi}^{min}$ the smallest $\dot{\phi}$.

Finally, for multidiving, the phase function reduction factor, ξ, is defined by the product of the three η,

$$\xi_j = \eta_j^{ex}\eta_j^{rp}\eta_j^{rg} = \frac{(\dot{\phi})_{max}}{(\dot{\phi})_j}\left[1 - \left(1 - \frac{\dot{\phi}^{min}}{\dot{\phi}}\right)\exp\left(-\lambda_m t_{j-1}\right)\right]\exp\left(-\lambda_r t_{j-1}^{cum}\right)$$

with t_{j-1} consecutive dive time, and t_{j-1}^{cum} cumulative dive time, as noted. Since bubble numbers increase with depth, reduction in permissible phase function is commensurate. Multiday diving is mostly impacted by λ_r, while repetitive diving mostly by λ_m.

• RGBM MODEL IMPLEMENTATIONS •

Two implementations exist. One is a Haldane folded algorithm using phase factors from the full iterative model to limit repetitive, reverse profile, multiday activities, and flying after diving. The folded version is found in many decometers on the market today. The full version is the basis of released mixed gas technical tables and simplified no-group, no-calc recreational air and nitrox tables up to 10,000 *ft* elevation. Meter implementations of the full RGBM are underway, following release of the full up RGBM EXPLORER by HydroSpace Engineering. Both modified and iterative RGBM are offered to users of GAP and ABYSS diveware. A special version of the RGBM will also be marketed over the Net to the diving user community (RGBMdiving.com).

Iterative RGBM Implementation

As detailed, the full RGBM employs a phase volume constraint across the total dive profile. The gel parameterization is replaced by flexible seed skins with appropriate EOS, permeable to gas diffusion at all pressures and temperatures. Gas diffuses across the bubble interface, and the bubble is subject to Boyle expansion-contraction.

The phase volume constraint equation is rewritten in terms of a phase function, ϕ, varying in time,

$$\int_0^\tau \frac{\partial \phi}{\partial t}\, dt \leq \Phi$$

with, as before,

$$\dot{\phi} = \frac{\partial \phi}{\partial t}$$

for Φ the separated phase, and τ some (long) cutoff time. More particularly, for Π the total gas tension,

$$\dot{\phi} = \left[\frac{\partial V}{\partial t}\right]_{diffusion} + \left[\frac{\partial V}{\partial t}\right]_{Boyle} + \left[\frac{\partial V}{\partial t}\right]_{excitation}$$

for,

$$\left[\frac{\partial V}{\partial t}\right]_{diffusion} = 4\pi DS \int_\varepsilon^\infty nr\left(\Pi - P - \frac{2\gamma}{r}\right)dr$$

$$\left[\frac{\partial V}{\partial t}\right]_{Boyle} = \int_\varepsilon^\infty n\left(\frac{T}{P}\frac{\partial}{\partial t}\frac{PV}{T}\right)dr$$

$$\left[\frac{\partial V}{\partial t}\right]_{excitation} = \frac{\partial}{\partial t}\left(4\pi\int_\varepsilon^\infty nr^2 dr\right)$$

with all quantities as denoted previously, and the bubble number integrand normalized,

$$\int_\varepsilon^\infty n\, dr = 1$$

From experiments, we employ an exponential representation in seed radii, one often seen in natural phenomena,

$$n = \beta^{-1}\exp(-\beta r)$$

To track Boyle bubble expansion-contraction easily, a set of multipliers, ξ, is tabulated in Table 1 below. For changes in pressure, we have,

$$\xi_i P_i V_i = \xi_f P_f V_f$$

as before, with i and f denoting initial and final states. Multipliers represent a 50/50 lipid-aqueous skin, following Sears, Adamson, and Epstein,

TABLE 1 - RGBM BOYLE MULTIPLIERS	
depth	EOS muliplier
(fsw)	ξ
30	0.610
90	0.732
150	0.859
210	0.939
270	1.032
330	1.119
390	1.169
450	1.183
510	1.203

The inherent unsaturation (oxygen window), υ, is given by *(fsw)*,

$$\upsilon = f_{O_2} P - 2.04(1 - f_{O_2}) - 5.47$$

with P ambient pressure, and f_{O_2} oxygen fraction. This window is assumed to take up inert gas under compression-decompression.

To track gas transfer across bubble boundaries, we need the mass transport coefficients, DS, for inert gases. Table 2 lists DS for the same 50/50 lipid-aqueous surface, using Frenkel, Bennett and Elliot, Harvey, Hirschfelder, and Batchelor,

TABLE 2 - RGBM MASS TRANSER COEFFICIENTS	
Gas	DS
	$\mu m^2/sec\ fsw \times 10^{-6}$
H_2	72.5
He	18.4
Ne	10.1
N_2	56.9
Ar	40.7
O_2	41.3

Notice that helium has a low mass transport coefficient, some three times smaller than nitrogen.

The phase function, ϕ, depends on number of bubbles, n, stimulated into growth by compression-decompression, the supersaturation gradient, G, seed expansion-contraction by radial diffusion, $\partial r/\partial t$, Boyle expansion-contraction, PV, under pressure changes, and temperature, T, in general. The excitation radius, ε, depends on the material properties, and is given for nitrogen (μm),
and for helium,

$$\varepsilon_{N_2} = 0.007655 + 0.001654 \left[\frac{T}{P}\right]^{1/3} + 0.041602 \left[\frac{T}{P}\right]^{2/3}$$

for T measured in absolute $K°$, and P given in *fsw*, as before, with ranges

$$\varepsilon_{He} = 0.003114 + 0.015731 \left[\frac{T}{P}\right]^{1/3} + 0.025893 \left[\frac{P}{T}\right]^{2/3}$$

for virial coefficients, aqueous to lipid materials, varying by factors of 0.75 to 4.86 times the values listed above. Both expressions above represent fits to RGBM mixed gas data across lipid and aqueous bubble films, and are different from other phase models. Values of excitation radii, ε, above range from 0.01 to 0.05 μm for sea level down to 500 *fsw*, compared to excitation radii in other models (varying permeability and tissue bubble diffusion models) which vary in the 1 μm range.

In the very large pressure limit, excitation radii (like beebees) are in the 1/1,000 μm range. Table 3 lists excitation radii (air) according to the RGBM.

TABLE 3 - REDUCED GRADIENT BUBBLE MODEL EXCITATION RADII			
pressure	excitation radius	pressure	excitation radius
P (*fsw*)	$\varepsilon(\mu m)$	P (*fsw*)	$\varepsilon(\mu m)$
13	0.174	153	0.033
33	0.097	183	0.029
53	0.073	283	0.024
73	0.059	383	0.016
93	0.051	483	0.011
113	0.046	583	0.009

Two parameters, closing the set, are nominally (STP),

$$\Phi = 840 \ \mu m^3$$

$$\beta = 0.6221 \ \mu m^{-1}$$

with,

$$2\gamma = 44.7\left[\frac{P}{T}\right]^{1/4} + 24.3\left[\frac{P}{T}\right]^{1/2} \quad fsw\ \mu m$$

FOLDED RGBM IMPLEMENTATION

The following is specific to ZHL implementation of the RGBM across critical parameters and nonstop time limits of the ZHL algorithm. Extensive computer fitting of profiles and recalibration of parameters to maintain the RGBM within the ZHL limits is requisite here. ABYSS has implemented this synthesis into Internet diveware. Deep stops, not intrinsic in this limited, still basically Haldane approach, can be inserted empirically. And this model can be imbedded in any *M*-value algorithm, or staging format. This was the first correlated (folded) application of the gradient factor method discussed later with deep stops.

Haldane approaches use a dissolved gas (tissue) transfer equation, and a set of critical parameters to dictate diver staging through the gas transfer equation. In the Workman approach, the critical parameters are called *M*-values, while in the Buhlmann formulation they are called *a* and *b*. They are equivalent sets, slightly different in representation but not content. Consider air, nitrox, heliox, and trimix in the ZHL formalism.

Air tissue tensions (nitrogen partial pressures), p, for ambient nitrogen partial pressure, p_a, and initial tissue tension, p_i, evolve in time, t, in usual fashion in compartment, τ, according to,

$$p - p_a = (p - p_a)\exp(-\lambda t)$$

for,

$$\lambda = \frac{0.693}{\tau}$$

with *t* tissue halftime, and, for air,

$$p_a = 0.79 P$$

and with ambient pressure, *P*, given as a function of depth, *d*, in units of *fsw*,

$$P = \eta d + P_0$$

Staging is controlled in the Buhlmann ZHL algorithm through sets of tissue parameters, *a* and *b*, listed below in Table 4 for 14 tissues, τ, through the minimum permissible (tolerable) ambient pressure, P_{min}, by,

$$P_{min} = (p - a)b$$

across all tissue compartments, τ, with the largest P_{min} limiting the allowable ambient pressure, P_{min}. Recall that 1 bar = 1.103 atm, 1 atm = 33 fsw as conversion metric between bar and fsw in pressure calculations. Linear extrapolations are often used for different sets of halftimes and critical parameters, a and b.

TABLE 4 - NITROGEN ZHL CRITICAL PARAMETERS (a,b)		
halftime	critical intercept	critical slope
τ (min)	a (bar)	b
5.0	1.198	0.542
10.0	0.939	0.687
20.0	0.731	0.793
40.0	0.496	0.868
65.0	0.425	0.882
90.0	0.395	0.900
120.0	0.372	0.912
150.0	0.350	0.922
180.0	0.334	0.929
220.0	0.318	0.939
280.0	0.295	0.944
350.0	0.272	0.953
450.0	0.255	0.958
635.0	0.236	0.966

In terms of critical tensions, M, according to the USN, the relationship linking the two sets,

$$M = \frac{P}{b} + a = \Delta M P - M_0$$

so that,

$$\Delta M = \frac{1}{b}$$

$$M_0 = a$$

in units of *bar*, though the usual representation for M is *fsw*. The above set, a and b, hold generally for nitrox, and, to low order, for heliox (and trimix too). Tuned modifications for heliox and trimix are also tabulated below.

Over ranges of depths, tissue halftimes, and critical parameters of the ZHL algorithm, approximately 2,300 dive profiles were simulated using both the RGBM and Haldane ZHL algorithms. To correlate the two as closely as possible, maximum likelihood analysis is used, that is, extracting the temporal features of three bubble parameters mating the RGBM and ZHL algorithms extending critical parameters of the ZHL Haldane model to more complete bubble dynamical framework. These factors, f, are described next, with their linkages to a and b, and are the well known *reduction factors* of the RGBM, or *gradient factors* in general.

According to the RGBM fits across the ZHL profiles (2,300), a correlation can be established through gradient factors, f, such that for any set of nonstop gradients, G,

$$G = M - P$$

a reduced set, G_f, obtains from the nonstop set, G, for multidiving through the reduction factors, $f \leq 1$,

$$G_f = fG$$

so that,

$$M_f = \frac{P}{b_f} + a_f = G_f + P = fG + P$$

but, since,

$$fG = f(M - P) = f\left[\frac{P}{b} + a - P\right]$$

we have,

$$a_f = fa$$

$$b_f = \frac{b}{f(1-b)+b}$$

The new (reduced) staging regimen is then simply,

$$P_{min} = (p - a_f)b_f$$

using *reduced* critical parameters, a_f and b_f. Certainly, as $f \to 1$, then $a_f \to a$, and $b_f \to b$, as requisite. Now all that remains is specification of f, particularly in terms of repetitive, reverse profile, and multiday diving, as limited by the bubble dynamical RGBM. The full factor, f, depends on tissue halftime, τ, generally through the relationship (for nitrox),

$$f = (1 - f_0)\frac{\tau}{180} + f_0 \qquad (f = 1, \tau \geq 180 \min)$$

as the tissue scaling up through the 180 *min* nitrogen compartment, with multidiving weighting,

$$f_0 = .45 f_{rp} + .30 f_{dp} + f_{dy}$$

where f_{rp}, f_{dp}, and f_{dy} are reduction factors for repetitive, reverse profile (deeper than previous), and multiday (time spans of 30 *hrs* or more) diving. These forms for multidiving f are dependent on time between dives, t_{sur}, maximum ambient pressure difference between reverse profile dives, $(\Delta P)_{max}$, maximum ambient pressure, P_{max}, and multiday diving frequency, n, over 24 *hr* time spans. Specifically, they are written,

$$f_{rp} = 1 - .45 \exp\left[-\frac{(t_{sur} - \eta_{rp})^2}{4\eta_{rp}^2}\right]$$

$$10 \min \leq \eta_{rp} \leq 90 \min$$

$$f_{dp} = 1 - .45\left[1 - \exp\left(-\frac{(\Delta P)_{max}}{P_{max}}\right)\right]\exp\left[-\frac{(t_{sur} - \eta_{dp})^2}{4\eta_{dp}^2}\right]$$

$$30 \text{ min} \leq \eta_{dp} \leq 120 \text{ min}$$

$$f_{dy} = .70 + .30 \exp\left(-\frac{n}{\eta_{dy}}\right)$$

$$12 \text{ hrs} \leq \eta_{dy} \leq 18 \text{ hrs}$$

with t_{sur} measured in *min*, and n the number of consecutive days of diving within 30 *hr* time spans. These factors are applied after 1 *min* of surface interval (otherwise, previous dive continuation). The difference, $(\Delta P)_{max}$, can be the time averaged difference between depths on the present and previous dives (computed on the fly). Reduction factors are consistent (folded in maximum likelihood in the RGBM) with the following:

1. Doppler bubble scores peak in an hour or so after a dive;
2. reverse profiles with depth increments beyond 50 *fsw* incur increasing DCS risk, somewhere between 5% and 8% in the depth increment range of 40 *fsw* - 120 *fsw*;
3. Doppler bubble counts drop tenfold when ascent rates drop from 60 *fsw/min* to 30 *fsw/min*;
4. multiday diving risks increase by factors of 2 - 3 (though still small) over risk associated with a single dive.

The standard set, a, b, and τ, given in Table 9 hold across nitrox exposures, and the tissue equation remains the same. The obvious change for a nitrox mixture with nitrogen fraction, f_{N_2}, occurs in the nitrogen ambient pressure, p_{aN_2}, at depth, d, in analogy with the air case,

$$p_{aN_2} = f_{N_2} P = f_{N_2}(d + P_0)$$

with P ambient pressure (*fsw*). All else is unchanged. The case, $f_{N_2} = 0.79$, obviously represents an air mixture.

The standard set, a, b, and τ is modified for helium mixtures, with basic change in the set of halftimes, τ, used for the set, a and b. To lowest order set, a and b for helium are the same as those for nitrogen, though we will list the modifications in Table 5 below. Halftimes for helium are approximately 2.65 times faster than those for nitrogen, by Graham's law (molecular diffusion rates scale inversely with square root of atomic masses). That is,

$$\tau_{He} = \frac{\tau_{N_2}}{2.65}$$

because helium is approximately 7 times lighter than nitrogen, and diffusion rates scale with square root of the ratio of atomic masses. The tissue equation is the same as the nitrox tissue equation, but with helium constants, λ, defined by the helium tissue halftimes. Denoting the helium fraction, f_{He}, the helium ambient pressure, p_{aHe}, is given by,

$$p_{aHe} = f_{He} P = f_{He}(d + P_0)$$

as with nitrox. Gradient factors are the same, but the tissue scaling is different across the helium set,

$$f = (1 - f_0)\frac{\tau}{67.8} + f_0 \qquad (f = 1, \tau \geq 67.8 \text{ min})$$

and all else is the same.

For trimix, both helium and nitrogen must be tracked with tissue equations, and appropriate average of helium and nitrogen critical parameters used for staging. Thus, denoting nitrogen and helium fractions, f_{N_2}, and f_{He}, ambient nitrogen and helium pressures, p_{aN_2} and p_{aHe}, take the form,

$$p_{aN_2} = f_{N_2} P = f_{N_2}(d + P_0)$$

$$p_{aHe} = f_{He} P = f_{He}(d + P_0)$$

Tissue halftimes are mapped exactly as listed in Tables 3 and 4, and used appropriately for nitrogen and helium tissue equations. Additionally,

$$f_{O_2} + f_{N_2} + f_{He} = 1$$

and certainly in Tables 3 and 4, one has the mapping,

$$\tau_{He} = \frac{\tau_{N_2}}{2.65}$$

TABLE 5 - HELIUM ZHL CRITICAL PARAMETERS (a,b)

halftime τ (min)	critical intercept a (bar)	critical slope b
1.8	1.653	0.461
3.8	1.295	0.604
7.6	1.008	0.729
15.0	0.759	0.816
24.5	0.672	0.837
33.9	0.636	0.864
45.2	0.598	0.876
56.6	0.562	0.885
67.8	0.541	0.892
83.0	0.526	0.901
105.5	0.519	0.906
132.0	0.516	0.914
169.7	0.510	0.919
239.6	0.495	0.927

Then, total tension, Π, is the sum of nitrogen and helium components,

$$\Pi = \left(p_{aN_2} + p_{aHe}\right) + \left(p_{iN_2} + p_{aN_2}\right)\exp\left(-\lambda_{N_2} t\right) + \left(p_{iHe} - p_{aHe}\right)\exp\left(-\lambda_{He} t\right)$$

with λ_{N_2} and λ_{He} decay constant for the nitrogen and helium halftimes in Tables 3 and 4. Critical parameters for trimix, α_f and β_f, are just weighted averages of critical parameters, a_{N_2}, b_{N_2}, a_{He}, b_{He}, from Tables 3 and 4, that is, generalizing to the reduced set, a_f and b_f,

$$\alpha_f = \frac{f_{N_2} a_{fN_2} + f_{He} a_{fHe}}{f_{N_2} + f_{He}}$$

$$\beta_f = \frac{f_{N_2} b_{fN_2} + f_{He} b_{fHe}}{f_{N_2} + f_{He}}$$

The staging regimen for trimix is,

$$P_{min} = (\Pi - \alpha_f)\beta_f$$

as before. The corresponding critical tension, M_f, generalizes to,

$$M_f = \frac{P}{\beta_f} + \alpha_f$$

Overall, the RGBM algorithm is conservative with safety imparted to the Haldane ZHL model through multidiving f factors. Estimated DCS incidence rate from likelihood analysis is 0.01% at the 95% confidence level for the overall RGBM. Table and meter implementations with consistent coding should reflect this estimated risk. Similar estimates and comments apply to the ZHL mixed gas synthesis.

• RESULTS AND COMPARISONS •

Here, we merely look at the coarse bases of both meter and diveware implementations of the RGBM algorithm, one with extended range of applicability based on simple dual phase principles. Haldane approaches have dominated decompression algorithms for a very long time, and the RGBM has been long in coming on the commercial scene. With recent technical diving interest in deep stop modeling, and concerns with repetitive diving in the recreational community, phase modeling is timely and pertinent.

Nonstop Comparisons

So, a next question is how does the RGBM compare with classical Haldane models as far as staging ascents, limiting multiexposures, and treating mixed gases? Generally, for short nonstop air diving, the RGBM reproduces the Spencer limits. For multidiving in spans shorter than 1 - 3 *hr*, the RGBM reduces nonstop limits by 10% to 20% depending on surface interval, depth, altitude, and duration of present and previous dive. Multiday diving is impacted to lesser degree. Some comparisons appear in Table 6 for three days of repetitive air diving (120 *fsw*/10 *min* twice a day with 45 *min* surface interval). Computer choices are illustrative, not indictive.

The RGBM (first dive) nonstop limits (depth/time) are roughly 150/6, 140/7, 130/9, 120/10, 110/13, 100/17, 90/22, 80/28, 70/36, 60/51, 50/69, and 40/120. In the mixed gas arena, Table 7 lists nonstop time limits

RESULTS AND COMPARISONS

TABLE 6 - NONSTOP LIMITS FOR RGBM AND HALDANE AIR MULTIDIVING

computer/algorithm	Dive 1	Dive 2	Dive 3	Dive 4	Dive 5	Dive 6
VYTEC, EXPLORER/RGBM	10	6	9	5	9	5
COBRA/Spencer	10	9	10	9	10	9
DATA PLUS/USN	12	6	12	6	12	6
DELPHI/USN	10	10	10	10	10	10
ABYSS/RGBM	6	6	6	6	6	6
DC12/ZHL	9	7	9	7	9	7
ALADIN/ZHL	8	8	8	8	8	8
ALADIN PRO/ZHL	10	7	10	7	10	7
SOURCE/USN	12	9	12	9	12	9

TABLE 7 - TRIMIX NONSTOP LIMITS FOR RGBM AND ZHL (HALDANE)

depth (fsw)	RGBM (min)	ZHL (min)
80	28	26
90	23	22
100	19	18
110	16	15
120	14	13
130	12	11
140	11	10
150	10	9

for ranged trimix, that is, 13% to 17% helium, 61% to 53% nitrogen, and 26% to 30% oxygen, according to RGBM and ZHL (Buhlmann).

These limits are used by NAUI Technical Diving for training purposes. While both sets of nonstop time limits are different in Tables 3 and 4, the more dramatic effects of the RGBM show up for deep staging, as seen in Table 8.

	TABLE 8 - DEEP SCHEDULES ACCORDING TO RGBM AND ZHL (HALDANE)					
stop	depth (fsw)	ZHL (min) (standard)	RGBM (min) (standard)	ZHL (min) (safer)	RGBM (min) (safer)
1	180	0	0	0	1
2	170	0	1	0	1
3	160	0	1	0	1
4	150	0	1	0	1
5	140	0	1	0	2
6	130	0	2	0	2
7	120	0	2	0	2
8	110	0	2	1	2
9	100	0	2	2	2
10	90	2	2	3	3
11	80	2	2	4	3
12	70	2	3	5	4
13	60	5	5	8	6
14	50	7	6	12	7
15	40	12	9	18	19
16	30	18	12	28	13
17	20	16	10	28	11
18	10	28	16	48	18
		93	77	147	98

Deep Comparisons

Comparative deep schedules for a trimix dive to 250 *fsw* for 30 *min* are contrasted, following a switch to air at 100 *fsw* and a switch to pure oxygen at 20 *fsw* on the way up. RGBM and ZHL are again employed, but with and without conservative safety knobs. In the case of ZHL, the outgassing tissue halftimes are increased by 1.5 in the conservative case, while for RGBM the bubble excitation radius is increased by 1.2 for comparison. Deeper stops are noticeably requisite in RGBM, but total decompression times are less than ZHL. The trimix is 33% helium, 51% nitrogen, and 16% oxygen.

Helium Comparisons

On most counts, helium appears superior to nitrogen as a diving gas. Helium bubbles are smaller, helium diffuses in and out of tissue and blood faster, helium is less narcotic, divers feel better when they leave the water after diving on helium, and helium minimum bends depths are greater than nitrogen minimum bends depths.

The first, in Table 9, is a comparison of enriched air and enriched heliair decompression diving, with a switch to 80% oxygen at 20 *fsw*. Dive is 100 *fsw* for 90 *min*, on EAN35 and EAH35/18 (nitrox 35/65 and trimix 35/18/47), so oxygen enrichment is the same. The decompression profile is listed in Table 9. Descent and ascent rates are 75 *fsw/min* and 25 *fsw/min*. Overall the enriched heliair decompression schedule for the dive is shorter than for the enriched air. As the helium content goes up, the decompression advantage for enriched heliair increases.

TABLE 9 - ENRICHED AIR AND HELAIR DECO PROFILE COMPARISON		
depth	enriched heliair EAH35/18 stop time	enriched air EAN35 stop time
(fsw)	*(min)*	*(min)*
100	90	90
30	2	4
20	5	7
10	12	11
	109	112

This may surprise you. But either way, now check out corresponding USN or ZHL decompression requirements for these dives. In the enriched heliair case, ZHL decompression time is 39 *min* versus 19 *min* above, and in the enriched air case, ZHL decompression time is 33 *min* versus 22 *min* above. This not only underscores helium versus nitrogen misfact in staging, but also points out significant differences in modern algorithms versus Haldane.

Lastly consider a deep trimix dive with multiple switches on the way up. Table 10 contrasts stop times for two gas choices at the 100 *fsw* switch. The dive is a short 10 *min* at 400 *fsw* on 10/65/25 trimix, with switches at 235 *fsw*, 100 *fsw*, and 30 *fsw*. Descent and ascent rates are 75 *fsw/min* and 25 *fsw/min*. Obviously, there are many other choices for switch depths, mixtures, and strategies. Below, the oxygen fractions were the same in all mixes, at all switches. Differences between nitrogen or helium, even for this short exposure, are nominal. Such usually is the case when oxygen fraction is held constant in helium or nitrogen mixes at the switch.

Gradient Factor Comparisons

It is also of interest to compare RGBM profiles against other strategies, particularly modern ones. An interesting comparison is seen in Tables 11, 13, and 14, contrasting decompression protocols for the RGBM with those of the Global Underwater Explorers (GUE) DPlan, a decompression planner offering ZHL gradient factor (GF) modifications, Haldane deep stops, and hybrids. The extent of validation of the DPlan models is unknown here. The gradient factor method, or juxtaposing of arbitrary multiplicative factors to Haldane gradients, $G = M - P$, has also been used by DPlan to induce deep stops on Haldane staging. Simple amplification of G in the deep zones will accomplish this.

The first (Table 11) is a 15/55 trimix (15% oxygen, 55% helium, and the rest nitrogen) dive to 250 *fsw* for 30 *min*. Descent rate is 99 *fsw/min*, and ascent rate is 33 *fsw/min*. A switch is made to EAN50 (50% nitrogen, 50% oxygen) at 70 *fsw*, and a final switch to pure oxygen is made at 20 *fsw*.

Down to the first switch onto EAN50, both models track roughly the same. After that, the DPlan calculation requires increasingly more decompression time as the stop depth decreases. This generally occurs when deep stops are juxtaposed onto Haldane staging. Time at depth incurs more decompression time in the shallow zone. This does not occur in the RGBM.

TABLE 10 - COMPARATIVE HELIUM AND NITROGEN GAS SWITCHES		
depth (fsw)	stop time *(min)* 10/65/25 *trimix*	stop time *(min)* 10/65/25 *trimix*
400	10.0	10.0
260	0.5	0.5
250	1.0	1.0
240	1.0	1.0
	18/50/32 *trimix*	18/50/32 *trimix*
230	0.5	0.5
220	0.5	0.5
210	0.5	0.5
200	0.5	0.5
190	1.0	1.0
180	1.5	1.5
170	1.5	1.0
160	1.5	1.5
150	1.5	2.0
140	2.0	1.5
130	2.0	2.5
120	4.0	4.0
110	4.5	4.0
	40/20/40 *trimix*	*EAN40*
100	2.5	2.0
90	2.5	2.0
80	2.5	2.0
70	5.0	4.0
60	6.5	5.5
50	8.0	6.5
40	9.5	7.5
	EAN80	*EAN80*
30	10.5	10.5
20	14.0	14.0
10	21.0	20.5
TOTALS:	116.0	108.0

TABLE 11 - DEEP TRIMIX RGBM AND DPLAN COMPARISON

depth (fsw)	RGBM time (min)	DPlan time (min)
250	30.0	30.0
170	0.5	
160	1.0	
150	1.0	1.0
140	2.0	2.0
130	2.5	2.0
120	2.5	2.0
110	2.5	3.0
100	4.0	3.0
90	5.5	6.0
80	6.0	6.0
70	2.5	4.0
60	3.0	5.0
50	6.0	7.0
40	6.5	8.0
30	9.0	15.0
20	12.0	19.0
10	17.0	35.0

Straightforward application of *ad hoc* gradient factors to the DPlan profiles in the deep zone can induce the deep stops shown. In the shallow zone, DPlan decompression times are more in step with conventional Haldane staging, that is, no gradient factor application and reduction of decompression times. Of course, in the shallow zone, gradient factors would need to be larger than one to reduce decompression times artificially over Haldane computed values. Wienke introduced them in folding the RGBM over the ZHL for repetitive, reverse profile, and multiday diving, and they all were less than one.

The gradient factor, γ, is applied to the (Haldane) fixed gradient, G, with resulting critical tension, M, as before.

$$M = \gamma G + P$$

for P ambient pressure. As γ gets large, or is increased beyond one, the required stop depth drops below the depth required for classical Haldane staging. Hence, a deep stop is imposed on the profile.

Roughly in applications,

$$0.40 \leq \gamma \leq 14.0$$

Though utilitarian to some, this begs the question of consistency and reproducibility across a spectrum of diving activities, except when folded over data.

Table 12 shows the RGBM decompression management spreadsheet, a standard software printout and compilation of profile data in terms of stops, times, depths, mixes, oxygen toxicity, and dive summary for the same dive.

A second deeper 10/70 trimix dive (10% oxygen, 70% helium, and the rest nitrogen) for 20 *min*, with an air switch at 220 *fsw*, and the same nitrox and oxygen switches at 70 *fsw* and 20 *fsw*, is tabulated in Table 13.

Here differences on air show more clearly, with the RGBM requiring more time at deep stops. In the shallow zone, RGBM times are shorter than DPlan, as before, with nitrogen washout in controlling tissue compartments dominating. Nitrogen bubbles are larger and more numerous for this dive according to the RGBM, and deeper stops for longer periods of time are thus requisite to control growth. A better strategy here might be to ride a helium mixture up to the 70 *fsw* zone, rather than switching to air at 220 *fsw*.

The final is an EAN28 (72% nitrogen, 28% oxygen) dive to 130 *fsw* for 90 *min*, with a switch to pure oxygen at 20 *fsw*. Ascent and descent rates are the same. Results are tabulated in Table 14.

Basic differences in the shallower zone again show here. The RGBM suggests less time on pure oxygen. These differences might be summarized as follows:

1. compared to others, the RGBM assigns realistic structures to the bubbles, tranfers gas across bubble surfaces, and accounts for Boyle expansion on ascent. Other bubble structures are often patterned after colloidal gels in the laboratory;
2. RGBM bubble seeds are 10 - 30 times smaller than other model seeds, and respond differently under pressure, and experience different dynamics;
3. compared to Haldane deep stop halving (first stop distance) and gradient factors, the RGBM is a model calculation from start to finish of the dive, and does not add additional time in the shallow zone because of greater dissolved gas buildup at the deep stops (incurring greater decompression debt in the shallow zone).

TABLE 12 - RGBM DECOMPRESSION MANAGEMENT SPREAD SHEET

Scaling/Control Flags

dive number = 1
rfac = 0.85
bfac = 0.46
surface consumption rate = 1.00 cubic ft/min
altitude = 0.0 ft
pfac = 1.00
unsat = 1

Dive Profile

time since last dive = 24000. min
time of last dive = 0.0 min
surface breathed nitrogen = 0.79   helium = 0.00
down switches = 2
switch 1 depth = 0.0 fsw   helium = 0.00   nitorgen= 0.79
speed = 99 fsw/min   way time = 0.0 min
switch depth 2 = 250 fsw   helium = 0.55   nitrogen = 0.30
speed = -33.0 fsw/min   way time = 30.0 min
r0 = 0.0346 microns   trimix = 0.55 helium,   0.30 nitrogen,
up switches = 2
switch depth 3 =70.0 fsw   helium = 0.00   nitrogen = 0.50
speed = -33.0 fsw/min   way time = 0.0 min
switch depth 4 = 20.0 fsw   helium = 0.0   nitrogen = 0.0
speed = -33.0 fsw/min   way time = 0.0 min
adjusted r0 = 0.0579 microns   d/gfac = 1.087   1.000

Decompression Schedule

bottom depth = 250.0 fsw
ppO_2 = 1.3 atm
OTU/CNS = 43.7 min/ 0.19%
bottom time = 32.5 min

REVERSE PROFILE COMPARISONS

Employing the RGBM and ZHL, we contrast model predictions for reverse profiles (RPs), extract underlying features and tendencies, and draw comparisons. Bubble and Haldane models overlap for short and shallow exposures. The observation has obviously been tendered that not much gas separates on short and shallow exposures, and then, bubble models should collapse to dissolved gas models in the limit. And 40 *fsw* for the reverse profile decrement, and 130 *fsw* depth have been suggested as limit points.

CONTINUED - TABLE 12 - RGBM DECOMPRESSION MANAGEMENT SPREAD SHEET

depth (fsw)	wait (min)	tissue (min)	tension (fsw)	pss (fsw)	ppO$_2$ (atm)	OTU (min)	CNS (%)	gas (ft^3)
250.0	30.0	-	-	-	1.3	43.7	0.19	2698
190.0	0.0	2.8	199.4	30.8	1.0	0.0	0.00	2
180.0	0.0	5.7	197.0	31.7	1.0	0.0	0.00	2
170.0	0.5	5.7	190.7	31.7	0.9	0.4	0.00	5
160.0	1.0	5.7	180.6	31.7	0.9	0.8	0.00	8
150.0	1.0	5.7	171.1	31.7	0.8	0.7	0.00	7
140.0	2.0	11.4	161.3	32.4	0.8	1.3	0.00	12
130.0	2.5	11.4	150.8	32.4	0.7	1.4	0.00	14
120.0	2.5	11.4	141.0	32.4	0.7	1.1	0.00	13
110.0	2.5	11.4	131.8	32.4	0.6	0.9	0.00	12
100.0	4.0	22.7	122.0	32.7	0.6	1.1	0.00	17
90.0	5.5	22.7	112.2	32.7	0.6	0.9	0.00	22
80.0	6.0	22.7	102.4	32.7	0.5	0.3	0.00	22
70.0	2.5	22.7	91.3	32.7	1.6	4.7	0.03	9
60.0	3.0	45.5	82.5	32.7	1.4	4.9	0.03	9
50.0	6.0	45.5	72.0	32.7	1.3	8.5	0.04	16
40.0	6.5	45.5	62.1	32.7	1.1	7.6	0.03	15
30.0	9.0	68.2	52.3	32.5	1.0	8.3	0.02	18
20.0	12.0	68.2	42.2	32.5	1.6	21.3	0.17	18
10.0	17.0	91.0	32.3	32.4	1.3	24.4	0.11	22
TOTALS:	83.5					132.4	0.64	510

deco plus surfacing time = 91.0 min
cum CNS% = 0.64   cum OTU = 132.4 min
cum gas consumption = 510. cubic ft
dive time = 93.5 min

When exposures are deeper and RP increments are greater than 40 *fsw*, model differentiations between dissolved gas and dual phase models appear in the staging regimens, as seen in Table 15, contrasting the ZHL and RGBM only for 160/40 and 40/160 RPs. Clearly phase models (RGBM) require deeper staging but shorter times, as seen in Table 15 for the surface intervals staggered as shown. The bottom times are 7 *min* and 100 *min* at 160 *fsw* and 40 *fsw* respectively in Table 15.

The Counterterror and Countermeasures Dive Team (CCDT) is involved in operations related to nuclear, chemical, and biological threats. Exercises and tests have yielded scattered data about RPs across a spectrum of breathing gas mixtures (nitrox, heliox, trimix). Recent activities have settled on trimix as the bottom and ascent gas, with pure

TABLE 13 - DEEPER TRIMIX RGBM AND DPLAN COMPARISON		
depth	RGBM time	DPlan time
(*fsw*)	(*min*)	(*min*)
300	20.0	20.0
190	0.5	1.0
180	0.5	1.0
170	0.5	1.0
160	0.5	1.0
150	1.0	1.0
140	1.0	1.0
130	1.5	1.0
120	1.5	1.0
110	1.5	1.0
100	2.0	1.0
90	2.0	1.0
80	2.5	3.0
70	2.5	3.0
60	3.0	4.0
50	4.0	5.0
40	6.0	8.0
30	9.0	11.0
20	8.0	14.0
10	12.5	27.0

TABLE 14 - DEEP NITROX RGBM AND DPLAN COMPARISON

depth (fsw)	RGBM time (min)	DPlan time (min)
130	90.0	90.0
70	0.5	1.0
60	5.5	5.0
50	7.0	8.0
40	13.0	14.0
30	17.5	22.0
20	10.5	15.0
10	20.0	25.0

TABLE 15 - COMPARATIVE ZHL AND RGBM DEEP RPs

Algorithm	Dive 1	Deco 1	Surface Interval	Dive 2	Deco 2
ZHL	160/7	10/3	30	40/100	none
RGBM		10/1			10/4
ZHL	40/100	none		160/7	10/11
RGBM		none			30/1, 20/1,10/2
ZHL	160/7	10/3	60	40/100	none
RGBM		10/1			10/3
ZHL	40/100	none		160/7	10/3
RGBM		none			20/1,10/2
ZHL	160/7	10/3	120	40/100	none
RGBM		10/1			10/2
ZHL	40/100	none		160/7	10/3
RGBM		none			20/1,10/1
ZHL	160/7	10/3	240	40/100	none
RGBM		10/1			10/1
ZHL	40/100	none		160/7	10/3
RGBM		none			20/1,10/1

oxygen breathed at 20 *fsw*. Mixtures range 13 - 40% helium, 44 - 64% nitrogen, and 16 - 30% oxygen. RP increments, Δd, vary from 40 - 120 *fsw*, and surface intervals are nominally greater than 60 *min*. The RGBM is the staging algorithm. Table 16 tabulates results of CCDT field activities,

TABLE 16 - CCDT RP RISK TABLE		
Dives	RP Increment (*fsw*)	Probable Hits
36	0 - 40	0
18	40 - 80	2
6	80 - 120	2

TABLE 17 - RGBM HELIOX DIVE EOS COMPARISON		
depth	RGBM aqueous stop time	RGBM lipid stop time
(*fsw*)	(*min*)	(*min*)
240	30.0	
150	1.0	1.0
140	2.0	2.0
130	2.0	2.0
120	3.0	3.5
110	3.0	3.0
100	3.0	3.5
90	3.0	3.5
80	3.5	4.0
70	6.5	7.0
60	6.5	7.0
50	6.5	7.5
40	10.0	11.0
30	10.5	12.5
20	14.0	16.0
10	19.0	23.5

with nominal surface intervals of an hour or more. Maximum bottom depth is 250 *fsw*, and exposures are near trimix NDLs. Dives are grouped in RP categories of 40 *fsw*.

The incidence rate, p, in Table 16 is 6.7%, with highest count in the 40 - 120 *fsw* increment range. There are many variables here, such as staging depth, gas mixture, exposure time, and surface interval not tabulated separately.

Practices for the deeper increments may border the yo-yo category, though no prior history of repetitive diving existed. Exercises continue, and data will grow. Trends are apparent in the above Table 16, but further analysis is required.

Extreme Diving Comparisons

Very deep (500 *fsw*), and very long and deep diving are extreme. In these scenarios, differences between phase models like the RGBM and classical dissolved gas models are pronounced. The 500 *fsw* dive by Ellyat on RGBM Tables has been reported in trade and technical diving magazines. More running summary follows in the next sections. But the 300 *fsw* jaunts for 4 - 5 *hrs* by the Woodville Karst Plain Project (WKPP) divers are something of wonder.

Figures 4 and 5 contrast real WKPP profiles against predictions of the ZHL and RGBM. RGBM and actual staging are right on. ZHL staging requires many more hours than necessary (actually dived). Note the multiplicity of gas switches to helium until the 70 *fsw* zone switch to EAN50.

EOS Comparisons

The RGBM accommodates lipid and aqueous skin structures for bubbles and seeds, through EOS material strength and gas transfer permeability. This has an impact on diver staging, as seen in Table 17 for limiting behavior of the EOS (lipid or aqueous). The comparison sample dive is a rebreather dive on heliox to 240 *fsw* for 30 *min*, with constant oxygen partial pressure, $ppO_2 = 1.3$ *atm*.

Effects of lipid or aqueous bubble skins start to show in the middle range in decompression stop times, increasing as depth decreases. Lipid structures are firmer than aqueous structures, and also less permeable to gas transfer. However, under Boyle expansion on ascent, lipid bubbles do not expand as much as aqueous ones.

FIGURE 4 - EXTREME WKPP DIVE VERSUS ZHL

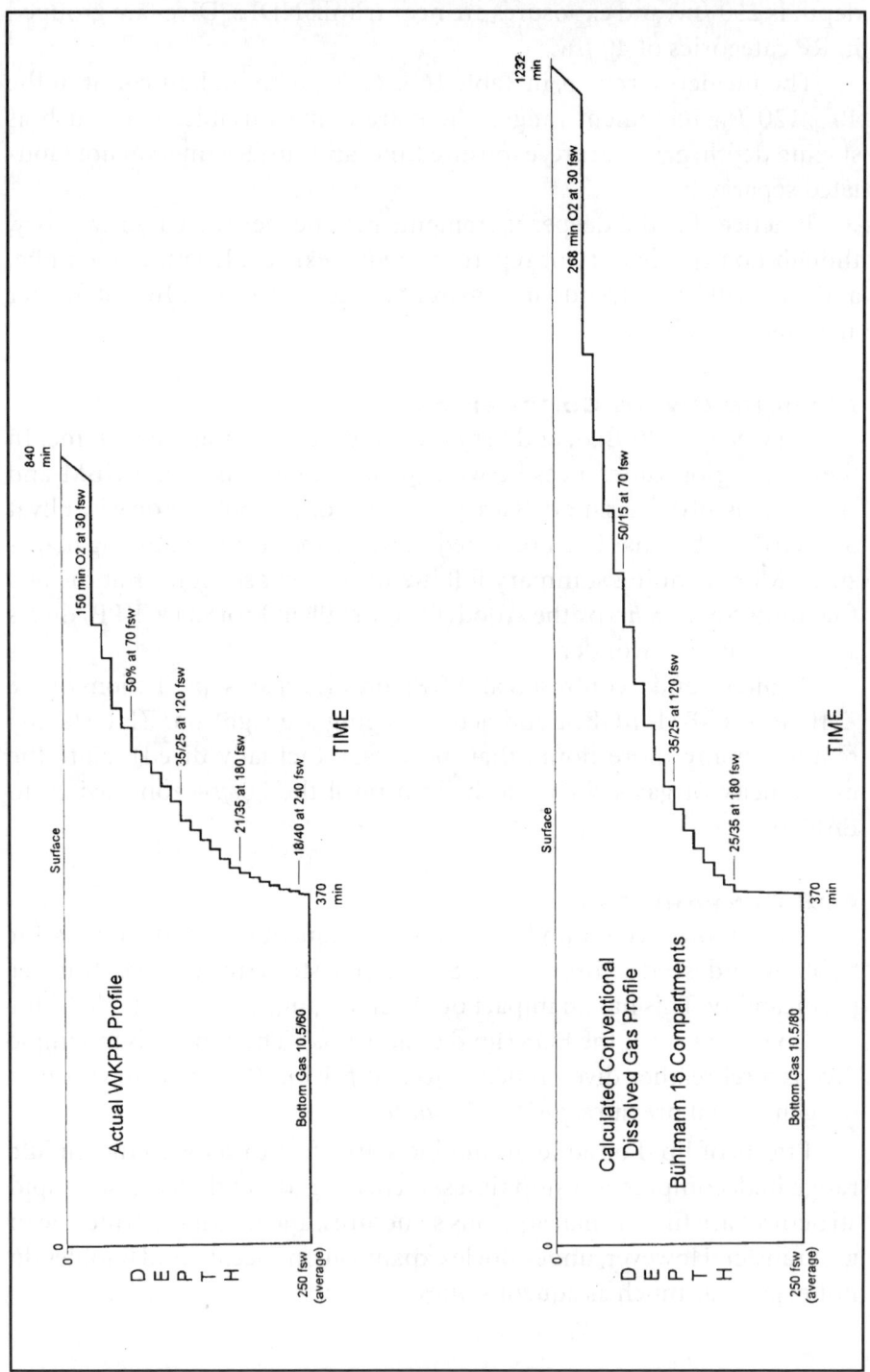

FIGURE 5 - EXTREME WKPP DIVE VERSUS RGBM

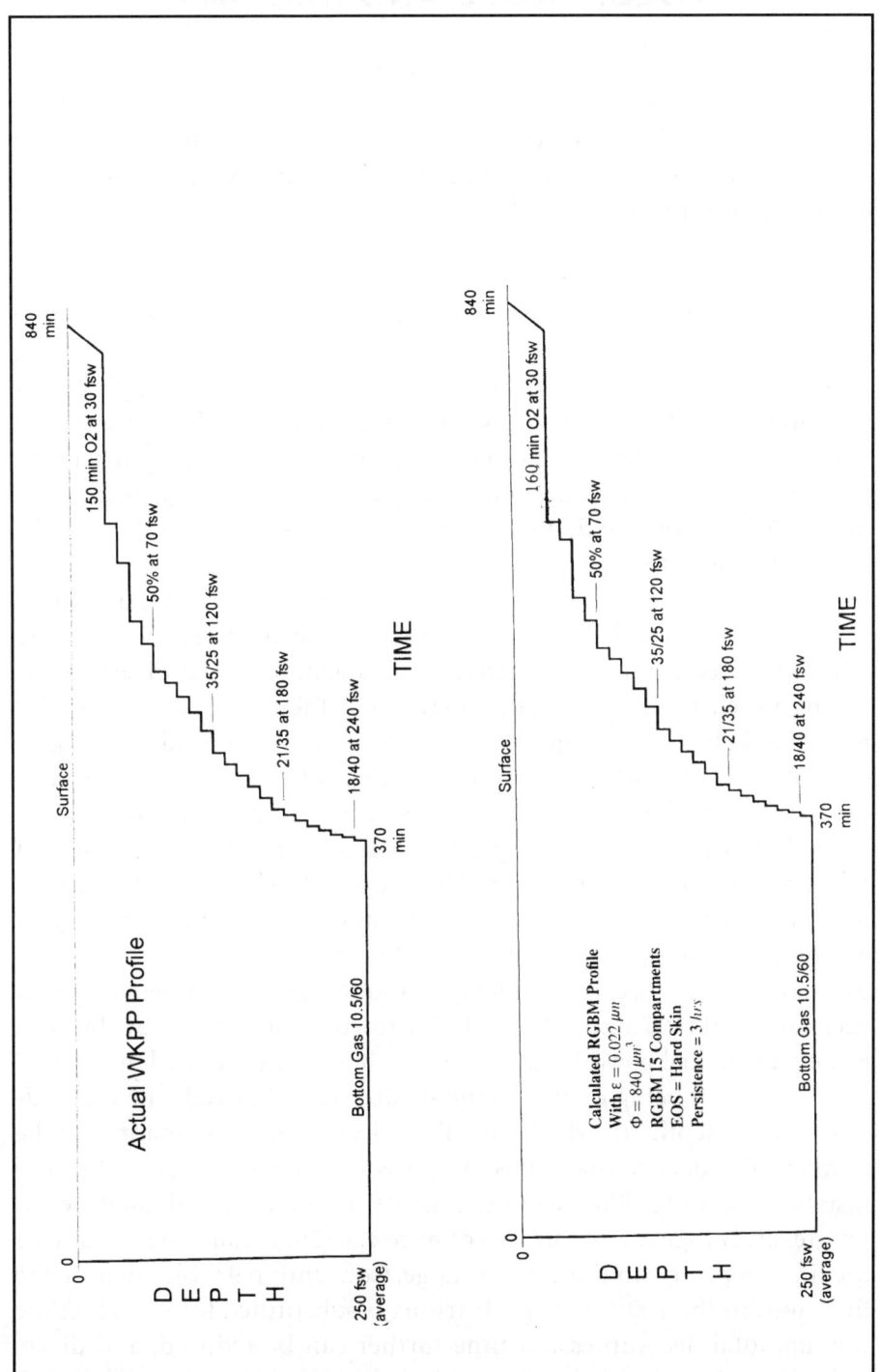

· DEEP STOPS AND HELIUM ·

Deep stops are what the name suggests, just decompression stops made at deeper depths than those traditionally dictated by classical (Haldane) dive tables or algorithms. They are fairly recent (last 15 years) protocols, suggested by modern decompression theory, but backed up by extensive diver practicum with success in mixed gas and decompression arenas, that is, technical diving. Tech diving encompasses scientific, military, commercial, and exploration underwater activities. The impact of deep stops has been a revolution in diving circles. So have slower ascent rates across recreational and technical diving. In quantifiable terms, slower ascent rates are very much akin to deep stops, though not as pronounced as decompression stops. Deep stops plus slow ascent rates work together. And they work together safely and efficiently, particularly when coupled to helium decompression strategies. The thermodynamic model of Hills was the first to incorporate deep stops naturally into the model staging regimens.

Deep stops usually reduce overall decompression time (hang time) too. And when coupled to the use of helium in the breathing mixture (trimix) to reduce narcotic effects of nitrogen, technical divers report feeling much better physically today when they leave the water. The reduction in hang time ranges from 10% to as high as 50%, depending on diver, mix, depth, and exposure time. Feeling better while decompressing for shorter periods of time is certainly a win-win situation that would have been thought an impossibility not too long ago. The basic tenets of Haldane decompression theory (neoclassical dissolved gas theory) postulate that deeper exposures (deep stop plus bottom time) incur greater offgassing penalties in the shallow zone. To see, check decompression tables based on Haldane methodology, and understand that such tables take no account of bubble growth in staging divers. But this is not seen in dual phase staging, where bubbles are prevented in the deep zone instead of being treated in the shallow zone à la Haldane methodology. The depth at which the first deep stops are made can be dramatically deeper than those required by conventional tables. For instance, a dive to 300 *fsw* on trimix for 30 *minutes*, with switches to progressively higher enrichments of nitrox at 120, 70, and 20 *fsw*, calls for the first deep stops in the 250 *fsw* range. Conventional tables require the first stops in the 100 *fsw* range. If trimix is substituted for nitrox on the way up, total decompression time further can be reduced, and divers today leave the water feeling better than they would on nitrox.

Deep Stops and Helium

For most early technical divers, obtaining deep and mixed gas decompression tables constituted one of many roadblocks to safe deep and exploration diving. Existing tables ranged from ultraconservative as an insulation against harm to a hodgepodge of protocols based on total misunderstanding. From this background, and driven by a need to optimize decompression schedules, deep stops steadily advanced as a safe and efficient change to diver staging. And this even though formal tests were usually not conducted in controlled environments, like hyperbaric chambers.

Deep Stop Strategies

Haldane originally found that deep stops were sometimes necessary in decompression formats and tests, but abandoned them, and could not incorporate them easily or naturally into a dissolved gas, critical tension (M-value) model on first principles. Nor can anybody these modern days. All he had to do was couple his dissolved gas dynamics to bubble dynamics. Deep stops do not emerge naturally in dissolved gas models. And Haldane didn't test deep enough either. Deep stops are patently a *deep* phenomena, whose utility and worth increase steadily with depth and exposure time.

Though deep stops are regarded as a major development in diving, the first experiments were more trial and error than scientific in nature. Just like so many other important developments in the real world. Underlying science with mechanistics would follow in the late '80s and '90s, and so with helium breathing mixtures.

Maybe "experiments" is too strict a description. Individuals, particularly in the cave diving community, toyed with decompression regimens in hopes of mimimizing their decompression time. The cave exploration Woodville Karst Plain Project (WKPP), mapping subsurface topographies in Florida, pioneered deep stop technology, establishing many rule-of-thumb protocols to be imposed on conventional tables. Irvine, Jablonski, and Mees stand at the forefront here, successfully conducting 6-hour dives at 280 *fsw* in the Wakulla cave complex with deep stop decompression times of 8.5 hours versus traditional Haldane hang times of 20 hours. Also, the horizontal penetrations of 19,000 *fsw* are world records (Guinness). Figures 5 and 6 sketch comparison profiles, along with mixtures, times, switch, and depths. Spectacular is a gross understatement. Certainly such contributions to diving science and spinoff model validation parallel Haldane a hundred years ago.

WKPP initially found that common decompression assumptions subject divers to extremely long decompression obligations, and ones that, regardless of their length, were inefficient. Divers also felt badly upon surfacing from extended decompression dives. Operationally (many dives over many years), WKPP divers found that the insertion of deep stops permitted shortening of shallower stops with an overall reduction in total decompression time. The decompression schedule was more effective, with effectiveness represented by subjective diver health and sense of well being. In so doing, WKPP also dispelled the voodoo helium myth as switches away from nitrox to trimix decompression schedules finalized after WKPP-testing-years. In lockstep mode, like (unpublicized) strategies developed in military, security, scientific, and even commercial sectors.

As discussed in previous chapters, there is science behind deep stops. The science is fairly simple. It's just a matter of how dissolved gases and bubbles behave under pressure changes. We used to think that controlling dissolved gas buildup and elimination in tissue and blood was the basis for staging divers and astronauts, and that bubbles didn't form unless dissolved gas trigger points were exceeded. At least that was the

FIGURE 6 - DUAL PHASE ELIMINATION

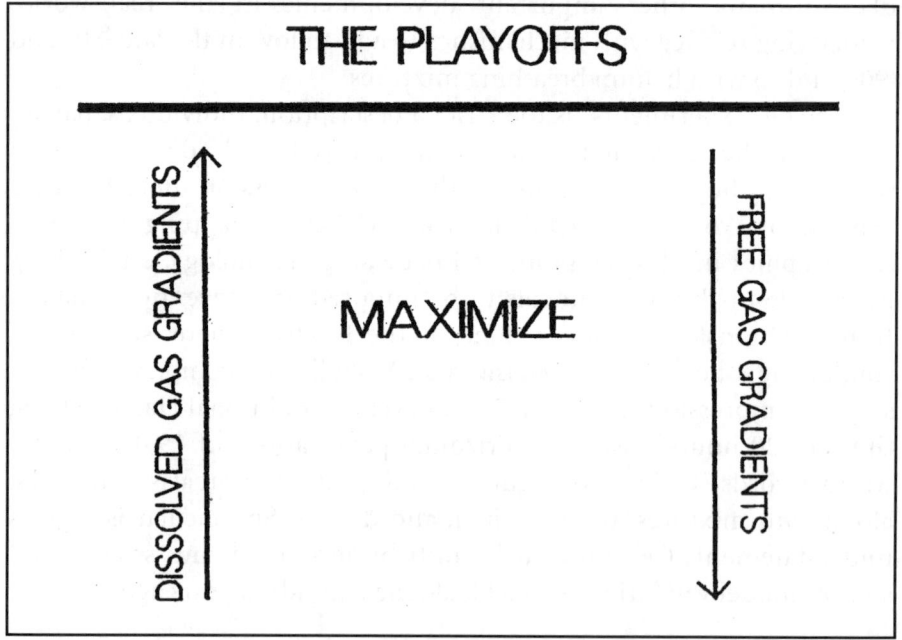

presumption that went into conventional (Haldane) tables. Chemists, physicists, and engineers never bought off on that. When silent bubbles were tracked in divers not experiencing any decompression problems, of course, this changed. And since bubbles need be controlled in divers, focus changed and switched from just dissolved gases to both bubbles and dissolved gases. Within such framework, deep stops emerge as a natural consequence. So do dual phase (bubbles plus dissolved gas) models.

To eliminate dissolved gases, the driving outgassing gradient is maximized by reducing ambient pressure as much as possible. That means bringing the diver as close to the surface as possible. But, to eliminate bubbles (gases inside them), the outgassing gradient is maximized by increasing ambient pressure as much as possible. That means holding the diver at depth when bubbles form. Deep stops accomplish the latter.

Clearly, from all the above, dominant modes for staging diver ascents depend upon the preponderance of free (bubbles) or dissolved phases in the tissues and blood, their coupling, and their relative time scales for elimination. This is now (will always be) a central consideration in staging hyperbaric or hypobaric excursions to lower ambient pressure environments. The dynamics of elimination are directly opposite, as depicted in Figure 6. To eliminate dissolved gases (central tenet of Haldane decompression theory), the diver is brought as close as possible to the surface. To eliminate free phases (coupled tenet of bubble decompression theory), the diver is maintained at depth to both crush bubbles and squeeze gas out by diffusion across the bubble film surface. Since both phases must be eliminated, depicted in Figure 7, the problem is a playoff in staging. In mathematical terms, staging is a *minimax* problem, and one that requires full blown dual phase models, exposure data, and some consensus of what is an acceptable level of DCS incidence.

Extreme WKPP divers make their first decompression stops at roughly 80% of actual dive depth for any dive. They dive helium exclusively, and the deep stop schedules they generate are not even remotely possible with air. WKPP schedules agree with reduced gradient bubble model calculations of the staging regimen, in both decompression profile shape and duration.

Other prescriptions for deep stops were imbedded in conventional tables. Something like this is employed, trial and error, and this one has been around for years in tech diving circles, sometimes attributed to Pyle, an underwater fish collector in Hawaii:

1. calculate your decompression schedule from tables, meters, or software;
2. half the distance to the first decompression stop and stay there a minute or two;
3. recompute your decompression schedule with time at the deep stop included as way time (software), or bottom time (tables);
4. repeat procedure until within some 10 - 30 ft of the first decompression stop;
5. and then go for it.

Within conventional tables, such a procedure was somewhat arbitrary, and usually always ended up with a lot of hang time in the shallow zone. Such is to be expected within dissolved gas decompression frameworks. So, deep stop pioneers started shaving shallow decompression time off their schedules, and jumped back into the water, picking up the trial and error testing where it left off. Seasoned tech divers all had their own recipes for this process. And sure, what works works in the diving world. What doesn't is usually trashed.

Deep Stop Models

Concurrently, full up dual phase models, spawned by the inadequacies and shortcomings of conventional tables, emerged on the diving scene. Not only did deep stops evolve self consistently in these models, but dive and personal computers put decompression scheduling with these new models in the hands of real divers. Real on-the-scene analysis and feedback tuned arbitrary, trial and error, and theoretical schedules to each other.

FIGURE 7 - COMPETING GAS TRANSFER PATHWAYS

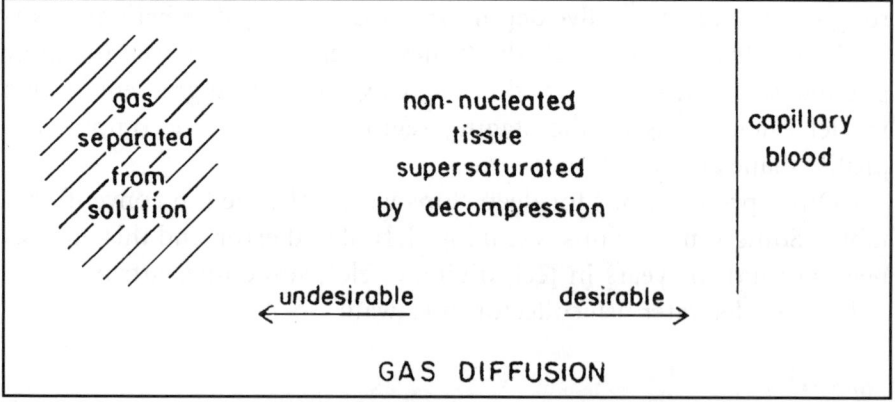

One thing common to all of these bubble models, as they are collectively referenced, is deeper stops, shorter decompression times in the shallow zone, and shorter overall decompression times. And they all couple dissolved gases to bubbles, not focusing just on bubbles or dissolved gas.

Details elsewhere, a few of the important ones can be summarized. The thermodynamic model of Hills really got the ball rolling, so to speak:
1. thermodynamic model (Hills, 1976) – assumes free phase (bubbles) separates in tissue under supersaturation gas loadings. Advocates dropout from decompression schedule somewhere in the 20 *ft* zone.
2. varying permeability model (Yount, 1986) – assumes preformed nuclei permeate blood and tissue, and are excited into growth by compression-decompression. Model patterned after gel bubbles studied in the laboratory.
3. reduced gradient bubble model (Wienke, 1990) – abandons gel parametrization of varying permeability model, and extends bubble model to repetitive, altitude, and reverse profile diving. Employed in recreational and technical diving meters, and basis for new tested NAUI tables;
4. tissue bubble diffusion model (Gernhardt and Vann, 1990) – assumes gas transfer across bubble interface, and correlates growth with DCS statistics. Probably employed in the commercial diving sector.

Not all these models have seen extensive field testing, but since they are all similar, earlier exposition, addressing testing and validation of the reduced gradient bubble model (RGBM), holds in broad terms. The 10,000s of tech dives on deep stops, of course, already validate deep stop technology and models to most, but the testing and validation described earlier spans deep stops to recreational diving in single model framework. And that is a very desired feature of any decompression theory and/or model. It almost goes without saying that models such as these have reshaped our decompression horizons, and will continue doing so.

LABORATORY EXPERIMENTS

One last item concerning deep stops remains, that is, laboratory experiments. Doppler and ultrasound imaging are techniques for detecting moving bubbles in humans and animals following compression-decompression. While bubble scores from these devices do not always correlate with the incidence of DCS, the presence or non-presence of bubbles is an important metric in evaluating dive profiles.

Neuman, Hall, and Linaweaver reported that Doppler scores of divers making deep stops on air dives to 230 *fsw* for 50 *minutes*, and 170 *fsw* for 30 *minutes*, were significantly lower (and statistically significant) than those of divers making conventional shallow stops for longer times than nominally required by conventional schedules. Lower DCS was also noted in the deep stop divers.

Analysis of more than 16,000 actual dives by Diver's Alert Network (DAN) prompted Bennett to suggest that decompression injuries are likely due to ascending too quickly. He found that the introduction of deep stops, without changing the ascent rate, reduced high bubble grades to near zero, from 30.5% without deep stops. He concluded that a deep stop at half the dive depth should reduce the critical fast gas tensions and lower the DCS incidence rate.

Marroni concluded studies with DAN's European sample with much the same thought. Although he found that ascent speed itself did not reduce bubble formation, he suggested that a slowing down in the deeper phases of the dive (deep stops) should reduce bubble formation. He will be conducting further tests along those lines.

Brubakk and Wienke found that longer decompression times are not always better when it comes to bubble formation in pigs. They found more bubbling in chamber tests when pigs were exposed to longer but shallower decompression profiles, where staged shallow decompression stops produced more bubbles than slower (deeper) linear ascents. Model correlations and calculations using the reduced gradient bubble model suggest the same.

Gerth, at NEDU, performing risk analysis for the USN, concluded deeper stops not only were necessary for Navy air and nitrox divers, but were also cost effective in terms of DCS risk versus time. Deep stop technology has developed successfully over the past 15 years or so. Tried and tested in the field, now some in the laboratory, deep stops are backed up by diver success, confidence, theoretical and experimental model underpinnings, and general acceptance by seasoned professionals.

Helium Strategies

Helium is a noble gas for deep diving, but was not always thought so. In the early days of technical and recreational diving, the use of helium for deep diving was discouraged, indeed, really feared. Based on misinformation and a few early problems in the deep diving arena, helium acquired a voodoo gas reputation, with a hands-off label.

Some misapprehension stemmed from the Hans Keller tragedy on helium mixes in 1962, some from misconceptions about isobaric switches à la light-to-heavy gases, some from tales of greater CNS risk, and some from a paucity of published and reliable decompression tables. Some concerns arose because 80/20 heliox no-decompression time limits (NDLs) for short and shallow dives were longer than air limits. So people assumed helium decompression was longer, and more hazardous, than nitrogen. In short, helium was getting a bad rap for a lot of wrong reasons.

It was also religion that switches from helium bottom mixtures to nitrogen should be made as early as possible, and that so doing would reduce overall decompression time the most. Not exactly so, at least according to modern decompression theory, and even classical Haldane theory if deep stops are juxtaposed on the profile. If helium and nitrogen are decreased in roughly same proportions as oxygen is increased until a big isobaric switch is made in the shallow zone to an enriched nitrox mix, decompression differences between early switches to nitrogen versus riding lighter helium mixes longer are small. Small according to modern decompression theory and practice, but more important, such helium protocols leave the decompression diver feeling better. As witnessed under field conditions, collective experiences of technical and scientific diving operations support that assertion today. So do modern decompression theories that have seen field testing, like the RGBM, and *ad hoc* deep stop protocols used by savvy divers.

Indeed there may be no need to switch to nitrogen mixtures at all. Riding helium mixtures to the surface with a switch to pure oxygen in the shallow zone can be decompression efficient, and safe too. So much so, that NAUI Technical Diving Operations has built a training regimen for divers and instructors based on helium for technical diving, and even offers a helitrox (enriched heliair) course. A full set of RGBM Tables supports helium-based training and tech diving.

In the same vein, the operational experiences of WKPP and LANL dive teams underscore many years of safe and efficient helium-based decompression diving. That couples to a modern revolution in decompression theory and practice. In fact, WKPP exploits on helium could fill a book. LANL too. NAUI Technical Diving has been utilizing helium-based training for the past three years or so without problems. All this means many, many 1,000s of tech dives with helium-based mixes.

Today, helium is proving its worth as a safe and reliable technical mix. Its use is changing technical and exploration diving. Exit deep air, and enter deep helium and deep stops. It seems about time, plus time for modern decompression theory to flush the dissolved gas theory entrenching diving for close to a century.

HELIUM DYNAMICS

The size of bubbles formed with various inert gases depends upon the amount of gas dissolved, and hence the solubilities. Higher gas solubilities promote bigger bubbles. Thus, helium is preferable to hydrogen as a light gas, while nitrogen is preferable to argon as a heavy gas. Neon solubility roughly equals nitrogen solubility. Narcotic potency correlates with lipid (fatty tissue) solubility, with the least narcotic gases the least soluble. Different uptake and elimination speeds suggest optimal means for reducing decompression time using helium and nitrogen mixtures. Following deep dives breathing helium, switching to nitrogen is without risk, while helium elimination is accelerated because the helium tissue-blood gradient is increased when breathing nitrogen. By gradually increasing the oxygen content after substituting nitrogen for helium, the nitrogen uptake can also be kept low. Workable gas switches depend on exposure and tissue compartment controlling ascent.

While light-to-heavy gas switches (such as helium to nitrogen) are safe and common practices, the reverse is not generally true. In fact, all heavy-to-light switches can be dangerous. In the former case, decreased tissue gas loading is a favorable circumstance following the switch. In the latter case, increased tissue gas loading can be disastrous. This is popularly termed the *isobaric* playoff.

Consensus among helium divers is that they feel better, less enervated, and subjectively healthier than when diving nitrogen mixtures. WKPP, LANL, and NAUI Technical Operations strongly attest to this fact. Though a personal and subjective evaluation, this remains very, very important. Physiological factors cannot be addressed on first principles always, and for some, just feeling better is good justification. Works for many. Postdive decompression stress on helium appears to be less than postdive nitrogen stress.

Another positive feature of helium diving underscores the minimum bends depth (MBD), that is, the saturation depth on a mix from which immediate ascension to the surface precipitates decompression sickness (DCS). For helium mixes, the MBD is always greater than that for proportionate nitrogen mix. For instance, the MBD for air (80/20 nitrox) is 33 *fsw*, while the MBD for 80/20 heliox is 38 *fsw*. This results from helium's lesser solubility compared to nitrogen with deeper and longer diving. It's a question of mass with transport.

Helium NDLs are actually shorter than nitrogen for shallow exposures, as seen comparatively in Table 18 for 80/20 heliox and 80/20 nitrox (air). Reasons stem from kinetic versus solubility properties of helium and nitrogen, and go away as exposures extend beyond 150 *fsw*, and times extend beyond 40 *min* or so.

Helium ingasses and outgasses 2.7 times faster than nitrogen, but nitrogen is 1.5 to 3.3 times more soluble in body aqueous and lipid tissue than helium. For short exposures (bounce and shallow), the faster diffusion rate of helium is more important in gas buildup than solubility, and shorter NDLs than nitrogen result. For long bottom times (decompression and extended range), the lesser solubility of helium is a

TABLE 18 - COMPARATIVE HELIUM AND NITROGEN NO DECOMPRESSION LIMITS		
depth	nitrox (80/20)	heliox (80/20)
(*fsw*)	NDL (*min*)	NDL (*min*)
30		
40	260	200
50	180	100
60	130	60
70	85	50
80	60	40
90	45	30
100	35	25
110	30	20
120	25	15
130	20	10
140	15	8
150	12	5
160	10	4
170	8	3

dominant factor in gas buildup, and helium outperforms nitrogen for staging. Thus, deep implies helium bottom and stage gas. Said another way, transient diving favors nitrogen while steady state diving favors helium as a breathing gas.

• RISK ANALYSIS AND VALIDATION •

Biological processes are variable in outcome. Correlations with outcome statistics are requisite to validate models against data. Often, this correlation is difficult to firmly establish (couple of percent) with fewer than 1,000 trial observations, while ten percent correlations can be obtained with 30 trials, assuming binomial distributed probabilities. For decompression analysis, this works as a disadvantage, because often the trial space of dives is small. Not discounting the possibly small trial space, a probabilistic approach to the occurrence of decompression sickness is useful and necessary. One approach, developed by Weathersby, and others for DCS analysis, called maximum likelihood, applies theory or models to diving data and adjusts the parameters until theoretical prediction and experimental data are in as close agreement as possible.

Risk Estimators

To perform risk analysis, a risk estimator needs to be employed. For diving, dissolved gas and phase estimators are useful. Two are used here. First is the dissolved gas supersaturation ratio, historically coupled to Haldane models, ϕ,

$$\phi = \kappa \frac{p - \lambda p_a}{p_a}$$

and second, ψ, is the separated phase, invoked by phase models,

$$\psi = \gamma \left[1 - \frac{r}{\xi} \right] G$$

For simplicity, the asymptotic exposure limit is used in the likelihood integrals for both risk functions,

$$1 - r(\kappa, \lambda) = \exp\left[-\int_0^\infty \phi(\kappa, \lambda, t)\, dt \right]$$

$$1 - r(\gamma, \xi) = \exp\left[-\int_0^\infty \psi(\gamma, \xi, t)\, dt \right]$$

with *hit - no hit*, likelihood function, Ω, of form,

$$\Omega = \prod_{k=1}^{K} \Omega_k$$

$$\Omega_k = r_k^{\delta_k} (1-r_k)^{1-\delta_k}$$

where, $\delta_k = 0$ if DCS does not occur in profile, k, or, $\delta_k = 1$ if DCS does occur in profile, k. To estimate κ, λ, γ, and ξ in maximum likelihood, a modified Levenberg-Marquardt algorithm is employed (*SNLSE*, Common Los Alamos Applied Mathematical Software Library), just a nonlinear least squares data fit (NLLS) to an arbitrary function (minimization of variance over K data points here), with $L1$ error norm. Additionally, using a random number generator for profiles across 1,000 parallel SMP (Origin 2000) processors at LANL, we construct 1,000 subsets, with $K = 2,000$ and $r = 0.006$, for separate likelihood regression analysis, averaging κ, λ, γ, and ξ by weighting the inverse variance.

RGBM Profile Risks

For recreational diving, both estimators are roughly equivalent, because little dissolved gas has separated into free phases (bubbles). Analysis shows this true for all cases examined, in that estimated risks for both overlap at the 95% confidence level. The only case where dissolved gas and phase estimators differ (slightly here) is within repetitive diving profiles. The dissolved gas estimator cues on gas buildup in the slow tissue compartments (staircasing for repets within an hour or two), while the phase estimator cues on bubble gas diffusion in the fast compartments (dropping rapidly over hour time spans). This holding true within all recreational diving distributions, we proceed to the risk analysis.

Nonstop limits (NDLs), denoted t_n, from the U.S. Navy, PADI, NAUI Tables, and Oceanic decometer provide a set for comparison of relative DCS risk. Listed below in Table 19 are the NDLs and corresponding risks (in parentheses) for the profile, assuming ascent and descent rates of 60 *fsw/min* (no safety stops). Haldane and RGBM estimates vary little for these cases, and only the phase estimates are included.

Risks are internally consistent across NDLs at each depth, and agree with U.S. Navy assessments. Greatest underlying and binomial risks occur in the USN shallow exposures. The PADI, NAUI, and Oceanic risks are all less than 2% for this set, thus binomial risks for single DCS incidence are less than 0.02%. PADI and NAUI have reported that field risks (p) across all exposures are less than 0.001%, so considering their enviable track record of diving safety, our estimates are liberal. Oceanic risk estimates track as the PADI and NAUI risks, again, very safely.

Next, the analysis is extended to profiles with varying ascent and descent rates, safety stops, and repetitive sequence. Table 20 lists nominal profiles (recreational) for various depths, exposure and travel times, and safety stops at 5 *msw*. Mean DCS estimates, r, are tabulated for both dissolved gas supersaturation ratio (ZHL) and bubble number excess (RGBM) risk functions, with, employing maximum variance, $r_\pm = r \pm 0.004$.

The ZHL (Buhlmann) NDLs and staging regimens are widespread across decompression meters presently, and are good representation for Haldane risk analysis. The RGBM is newer and more modern (and more physically correct), and is coming online in decometers and associated software. For recreational exposures, the RGBM collapses to a Haldane dissolved gas algorithm. This is reflected in the risk estimates above, where estimates for both models differ little.

Simple comments hold for the analyzed profile risks. The maximum relative risk is 0.0232 for the 3 dive repetitive sequence according to the Haldane dissolved risk estimator. This translates to 0.2% binomial risk, which is comparable to the maximum NDL risk for the PADI, NAUI, and Oceanic NDLs. Again, this type of dive profile is common, practiced daily on liveaboards, and benign. According to Gilliam, the absolute incidence rate for this type of diving is less than 0.02%. Again, our analysis overestimate risk.

Effects of slower ascent rates and safety stops are noticeable at the 0.25% to 0.5% level in relative surfacing risk. Safety stops at 5 *m* for 3 *min* lower relative risk an average of 0.3%, while reducing the ascent rate from 18 *msw/min* to 9 *msw/min* reduces relative risk an average of 0.35%.

Staging, NDLs, and constraints imposed by decometer algorithms are consistent with acceptable and safe recreational diving protocols. Estimated absolute risk associated across all ZHL NDLs and staging regimens analyzed herein is less than 0.232%, probably much less in actual practice. That is, we use $p = 0.006$, and much evidence suggests $p < 0.0001$, some ten times safer.

RISK ANALYSIS AND VALIDATION

TABLE 19 - RISK ESTIMATES FOR VARIOUS NDLs

d (fsw)	USN t_n (min)	PADI t_n (min)	NAUI t_n (min)	Oceanic t_n (min)
35	310 (4.3%)	205 (2.0%)		181 (1.3%)
40	200 (3.1%)	140 (1.5%)	130 (1.4%)	137 (1.5%)
50	100 (2.1%)	80 (1.1%)	80 (1.1%)	80 (1.1%)
60	60 (1.7%)	55 (1.4%)	55 (1.4%)	57 (1.5%)
70	50 (2.0%)	40 (1.2%)	45 (1.3%)	40 (1.2%)
80	40 (2.1%)	30 (1.3%)	35 (1.5%)	30 (1.3%)
90	30 (2.1%)	25 (1.5%)	25 (1.5%)	24 (1.4%)
100	25 (2.1%)	20 (1.3%)	22 (1.4%)	19 (1.2%)
110	20 (2.2%)	13 (1.1%)	15 (1.2%)	16 (1.3%)
120	15 (2.0%)	13 (1.3%)	12 (1.2%)	13 (1.3%)
130	10 (1.7%)	10 (1.7%)	8 (1.3%)	10 (1.7%)

TABLE 20 - DISSOLVED AND SEPARATED PHASE RISK ESTIMATES FOR NOMINAL PROFILES

profile (depth/time)	descent rate (msw/min)	ascent rate (msw/min)	safety stop (depth/time)	risk r_{RGBM}	risk r_{ZHL}
14 msw/38 min	18	9	5 msw/3 min	.0034	.0062
19 msw/38 min	18	9	5 msw/3 min	.0095	.0110
28 msw/32 min	18	9		.0200	.0213
37 msw/17 min	18	9	5 msw/3 min	.0165	.0151
18 msw/31 min	18	9	5 msw/3 min	.0063	.0072
18 msw/31 min	18	9		.0088	.0084
18 msw/31 min	18	18		.0101	.0135
18 msw/31 min	18	18	5 msw/3 min	.0069	.0084
17 msw/32 min SI 176 min	18	9	5 msw/3 min		
13 msw/37 min SI 174 min	18	9	5 msw/3 min		
23 msw/17 min	18	18	5 msw/3 min	.0127	.0232

RGBM Profile Data Bank

Divers using RGBM are reporting their profiles to a Data Bank, located at NAUI Technical Diving Operations (RGBMdiving.com). The information requested is simple:
1. bottom mix, depth, and time (square wave equivalent);
2. ascent and descent rates;
3. stage and decompression mixes, depths, and times;
4. surface intervals;
5. time to fly;
6. diver age, weight, and sex;
7. outcome (health problems).

This information aids in further validation and extension of model application space. Approximately 1,700 profiles now reside in the RGBM Data Bank. These profiles come from the technical diving community at large, essentially mixed gas, extended range, decompression, and extreme diving. Profiles from the recreational community are not included, unless they involve extreme exposures on air or nitrox (many repetitive dives, deeper than 150 *fsw*, altitude exposures, etc.). The RGBM, seen in Tables 14 and 15, is validated by risk analysis for nominal recreational diving.

RGBM Field Testing

Models need field validation and testing. Often, strict chamber tests are not possible, economically nor otherwise, and models employ a number of benchmarks and regimens to underscore viability. The following are some supporting the RGBM phase model and (released) nitrox, heliox, and trimix diving tables, meters, and software. These profiles are recorded in the RGBM Data Bank, and represent a random sampling and dive count over the full base.
1. counterterror and countermeasures (LANL) exercises have used the RGBM (full up iterative deep stop version) for a number of years, logging some 700 dives on mixed gases (trimix, heliox, nitrox) without incidence of DCS – 35% were deco dives, and 25% were repets (no deco) with at least 2 *hr* SIs, and in the forward direction (deepest dives first);
2. NAUI Technical Diving has been diving the deep stop version for the past 4 yrs, some estimated 1200 dives, on mixed gases down to 250 *fsw*, without a single DCS hit. Some 15 divers, late 1999, in France used the RGBM to make 2 mixed gas dives a day, without mishap, in cold water and rough seas. Same thing in the warm waters of Roatan in 2000 thru 2003;

3. NAUI Worldwide released a set of no-group, no-calc, no-fuss RGBM Tables for air, EAN32, and EAN36 recreational diving, from sea level to 10,000 *ft*, a few years ago. Minimum SIs of 1 *hour* are supported for repetitive diving in all Tables, and safety stops for 3 *minutes* in the 15 *fsw* zone are required always. Tables were tested by NAUI over a 3-year period without mishap;
4. modified RGBM recreational algorithms (Haldane imbedded with bubble reduction factors limiting reverse profile, repetitive, and multiday diving), as coded into Suunto, Mares, Dacor, ABYSS, HydroSpace, Plexus decometers, lower and already low DCS incidence rate of approximately 1/10,000 or less. More RGBM decompression meters, including mixed gases, are in the works;
5. a cadre of divers and Instructors in mountainous New Mexico, Utah, and Colorado have been diving the modified (Haldane imbedded again) RGBM at altitude, an estimated 650 dives, without peril. Again, not surprising since the altitude RGBM is slightly more conservative than the usual Cross correction used routinely up to about 8,000 *ft* elevation, and with estimated DCS incidence less than 1/10,000;
6. within decometer implementations of the RGBM, not a single DCS hit has been reported in nonstop and multidiving categories, beyond 300,000 dives or more, up to now;
7. extreme chamber tests for mixed gas RGBM are in the works, and less stressful exposures will be addressed – "extreme" here means 300 *fsw* and beyond;
8. probabilistic decompression analysis of some selected RGBM profiles, calibrated against similar calculations of the same profiles by Duke, help validate the RGBM on computational bases, suggesting the RGBM has no more risk than other models (Weathersby, Vann, Gerth methodology at USN and Duke);
9. all divers and Instructors using RGBM decometers, tables, or NET software have been advised to report individual profiles to DAN Project Dive Exploration (Vann, Gerth, Denoble and others at Duke);
10. ABYSS is a NET software package that offers the modified RGBM (folded over the Buhlmann ZHL) and, especially, the full up, deep stop version for any gas mixture, has a fairly large contingent of tech divers already using the RGBM and has not received any reports of DCS;
11. outside of proprietary (commercial) and RGBM Tables, mixed gas tables are a smorgasbord of less applicable Haldane dynamics and

stop insertions, as witnessed by the collective comments of the technical diving community;
12. extreme WKPP profiles in the 300 *fsw* range on trimix were used to calibrate the full RGBM. WKPP profiles are the most impressive application of RGBM staging, with as much as 12 *hours* less decompression time for WKPP helium-based diving on RGBM schedules versus Haldane schedules;
13. Ellyat, a TDI Instructor, dived the Baden in the North Sea to 520 *fsw* on RGBM Tables on two different occasions, and is planning a 500 *fsw* dive to an Andros Blue Hole with RGBM scheduling. In the North Sea dives, 3 *hours* were shaved off conventional hang time by RGBM application;
14. NAUI Worldwide released sets of deep stop RGBM nitrox, heliox, and trimix technical and recreational Tables that have been tested by NAUI Technical Diving Operations over the past 5 years, with success and no reported cases of DCS, for open circuit regulators and rebreathers;
15. Doppler and imaging tests in the laboratory, and analyses by Bennett, Marroni, Brubakk and Wienke, and Neuman, all suggest reduction in free phase counts with RGBM staging;
16. Gozum, a DAN diving doctor, performed 37 repetitive air dives over 7 days, out to the NDLs, using the Suunto/VYTEC RGBM implementation, and also reported feeling better than on pure Haldane schedules;
17. Freauf, a Navy SEAL in Hawaii, logged 20 trimix decompression dives beyond 250 *fsw* on consecutive days using RGBM Tables (pure oxygen switch at 20 *fsw*);
18. Scorese, a NAUI Instructor, and his students made 34 dives on the Andrea Doria with rebreathers and RGBM (constant ppO_2) Tables on nitrogen and trimix diluents. Aborted dives employed RGBM (open circuit) Tables as bailouts, and witnessed no mishaps.
19. Gerth, a USN researcher, reports deeper stops are necessary, and cost effective in terms of time and risk, for Navy air and nitrox divers.

Because DCS is binomially distributed in incidence probability, many trials are often needed (or other close profiles) to fully validate any model at the 1% level. Additionally, full validation requires DCS incidences, the higher the number, the better, contrary to desired dive outcomes.

· SUMMARY ·

The RGBM departs from other models in a number of ways, abandoning laboratory media parameterizations. Colloidal suspensions, such as gel, are far different than aqueous and lipid materials coating bubbles and seeds in the body. Additionally, typical gel-type micronuclei, with persistence time scales of tens of hours to days, have never been found in the body in any circumstance. Present wisdom suggests that seeds are produced by tribonucleation (tissue friction). The full-blown RGBM treats coupled perfusion-diffusion transport as a two-step flow process, with blood flow (perfusion) serving as a boundary condition for tissue gas penetration by diffusion. Depending on time scales and rate coefficients, one or another (or both) processes dominate the exchange. However, for most meter implementations, perfusion is assumed to dominate, simplifying matters and permitting online calculations. Additionally, tissues and blood are naturally undersaturated with respect to ambient pressure at equilibration through the mechanism of biological inherent unsaturation (oxygen window), and the model includes this debt in calculations.

The RGBM assumes that a size distribution of seeds (potential bubbles) is always present, and that a certain number is excited into growth by compression-decompression. An iterative process for ascent staging is employed to control the inflation rate of these growing bubbles so that their collective volume never exceeds a phase volume limit point. Gas mixtures of helium, nitrogen, and oxygen contain bubble distributions of different sizes, but possess the same phase volume limit point.

The RGBM postulates bubble seeds with lipid or aqueous skin structure. Bubble skins are assumed permeable under all crushing pressure. The size of seeds excited into growth is inversely proportional to the supersaturation gradient. At increasing pressure, bubble seeds permit gas diffusion at a slower rate. The model assumes bubble skins are stabilized by surfactants over calculable time scales, producing seeds that are variably persistent in the body. Bubble skins are probably molecularly activated, complex biosubstances found throughout the body. Whatever the formation process, the model assumes the size distribution is exponentially decreasing in size, that is, more smaller seeds than larger seeds in exponential proportions. The RGBM also employs an equation-of-state for the skin surfactants, linked to lipid and aqueous biophysical structures. Gas diffusion across the bubble film interface, and Boyle expansion and contraction under ambient pressure change are also tracked in the RGBM. The iterative (full up) RGBM has been implemented in the HydroSpace EXPLORER, and other implementations are underway. GAP is building an RGBM Palm Pilot.

In tracking seed excitation and number, gas transport into and out of bubbles, and Boyle-like expansion and contraction under pressure changes, the RGBM incorporates a spectrum of tissue compartments, ranging from 1 *min* to 480 *min*, depending on gas mixture (helium, nitrogen, oxygen). Phase separation and bubble growth in all compartments is a central focus in calculations, over appropriate time scales, and the model uses nonstop time limits tuned to recent Doppler measurements, conservatively reducing them along the lines originally suggested by Spencer (and others), but within the phase volume constraint.

The Haldane folded RGBM reduces the phase volume limit in multidiving by considering free phase elimination and buildup during surface intervals, depending on altitude, time, and depth of previous profiles. Repetitive, multiday, and reverse profile exposures are tracked and impacted by critical phase volume reductions over appropriate time scales. The model generates bubble seed distributions on time scales of minutes to hours, adding new bubbles to existing bubbles in calculations. Phase volume limit points are also reduced by the added effects of new bubbles. In the Haldane folded algorithm, deep stops can be injected into staging procedures with a simple time-depth scaling law correlated with calculations from the full iterative RGBM model.

The modified (folded) RGBM extends the classical Haldane model to repetitive diving by conservatively reducing the gradients, G. A conservative set of bounce gradients, G, can always be used for multiday and repetitive diving, provided they are multiplicatively reduced by a set of bubble factors, all less than one. Three bubble factors reduce the driving gradients to maintain the phases volume constraint. The first bubble factor reduces G to account for creation of new stabilized micronuclei over time scales of days. The second factor accounts for additional micronuclei excitation on reverse profile dives. The third bubble factor accounts for bubble growth over repetitive exposures on time scales of hours.

The RGBM (both versions) is a diveware implementation, accessible on the Internet at various sites. Additionally, the RGBM has been encoded into a number of commercial decompression meter products. Specific comparisons between RGBM and Haldane predictions for staging were summarized, with resultants generic for phase versus dissolved gas models. NAUI uses RGBM Tables for trimix, helitrox, nitrox, and altitude dive training.

The RGBM has witnessed testing and validation across technical and recreational diving sectors the past five years or so, and its record is exemplary. Deep stops with shorter overall decompression times, and the use of helium for extended exposures are revolutions of sorts in the technical diving community. The RGBM promotes both naturally and on first principles, because of coupled free and dissolved gas phase treatments.

An RGBM Data Bank has been established for mixed gas and decompression diving, plus extreme recreational air and nitrox, plus altitude exposures. Profiles stored in the Bank are used to extend the RGBM validation envelope, certify risk analysis, and offer technical divers information on actual exposure profiles. Check out the RGBM website at "RGBMdiving.com".

In addition to GAP and ABYSS, a special no frills, downloadable version of RGBM is available at the RGBM site (RGBMdiving.com) with decompression papers, RGBM Tables, and related information. Hope it's useful, and that this RGBM monograph is helpful to all.

NOTES

· APPENDIX ·

DIVE TABLE — AIR
Sea Level to 2,000 ft •	**78**
2,000 to 6,000 ft •	**79**
6,000 to 10,000 ft •	**80**

DIVE TABLE — EAN 32
Sea Level to 2,000 ft •	**81**
2,000 to 6,000 ft •	**82**
6,000 to 10,000 ft •	**83**

DIVE TABLE — EAN 36
Sea Level to 2,000 ft •	**84**
2,000 to 6,000 ft •	**85**
6,000 to 10,000 ft •	**86**

Reduced Gradient Bubble Model (RGBM)
Dive Table - Air
Sea Level to 2,000 ft / 610 m

DIVE ONE			DIVE TWO			DIVE THREE		
MAX DEPTHS		MDT	MAX DEPTHS		MDT	MAX DEPTHS		MDT
fsw	msw	minutes	fsw	msw	minutes	fsw	msw	minutes
130	40	10	80	24	30	30	9	150
120	36	13	75	23	30	30	9	150
110	33	16	70	21	40	30	9	150
100	30	20	65	20	40	30	9	150
90	27	25	60	18	55	30	9	150
80	24	30	55	17	55	30	9	150
70	21	40	50	15	80	30	9	150
60	18	55	45	14	80	30	9	150
50	15	80	40	12	110	30	9	150
40	12	110	35	11	110	30	9	150
30	9	150	30	9	150	30	9	150

This table is designed for scuba dives employing air.

Read the instructions and seek proper training before using this table or compressed air. Even strict compliance with this table will not guarantee avoidance of decompression sickness.

RGBM Air Dive Table
Sea Level to 2,000 ft / 610 m

Abbreviation Key
fsw = feet seawater   msw = meters seawater   MDT = Maximum Dive Time
SIT = Surface Interval Time DCS = Decompression Sickness   fpm = feet per minute
                             mpm = meters per minute

Rules for Table Use
- Depth measuring devices may require correction for use at altitude and in fresh water to determine a diveŕs actual dive depths and ascent/descent rates.
- Find your first diveís maximum depth in fsw or msw in the left two columns (Dive One). Follow that row to the right to get your MDT for Dive One and continue to the next columns under Dive Two to determine permitted repetitive depth and MDT for your second dive. Continue to the next columns under Dive Three to determine repetitive depth and MDT for your third dive.
- A minimum SIT of 1:00 hour is required between dive one and dive two and dive three.
- If your actual dive depth is not listed, use the MDT for the next greater depth listed.
- Dive Two may be shallower, but cannot exceed depth and MDT to the immediate right and on the same row as Dive One. Dive Three may be shallower than the depth listed but may not exceed the MDT in column three.
- The maximum descent rate on all dives is 75 fpm (23 mpm).
- The maximum ascent rate is 30 fpm (9 mpm).
- All dives require a safety stop at about 15 fsw (5 msw) (+/- 3 feet or 1 meter) for 3 minutes.
- No more than three repetitive dives within a 12 hour period.
- After a single dive in an 18-hour period wait a minimum of 12 hours before flying or ascending to an altitude greater than 8,000 feet/2438 meters. After two dives wait 15 hours and after three dives wait 18 hours.
- Inverted depth profiles (a shallow dive followed by a deeper dive) and mandatory staged decompression dives are not permitted while using this table.
- If you accidentally exceed your MDT cease all diving activities for 24 hours. If exceeded by less than 5 minutes, conduct a decompression stop at about 15 fsw (5 msw) for 6 minutes; if exceeded by 5 to 10 minutes, stop at about 15 fsw (5 msw) for 9 minutes before surfacing.
- If symptoms of DCS manifest breathe oxygen and evacuate to the nearest recompression facility.
- Example 1: Dive 1 to 130 fsw (40 msw) for 10 minutes, followed by a 1:00 SIT: followed by Dive 2 to 80 fsw (24 msw) for 25 minutes; followed by a 1:00 SIT; followed by Dive 3 to 30 fsw (9 msw) for 150 minutes.
- Example 2: Dive 1 to 115 fsw (35 msw) for 10 minutes followed by a 1:30 minute SIT; followed by Dive 2 to 71 fsw (22 msw) for 25 minutes; followed by a 1:45 SIT; followed by Dive 3 to 25 fsw (8 msw) for 120 minutes.

NAUI Worldwide Copyright © 2001. All rights reserved.

APPENDIX

DIVE SAFETY THROUGH EDUCATION

Reduced Gradient Bubble Model (RGBM)
Dive Table - Air
2,000 to 6,000 ft / 610 to 1829 m

DIVE ONE			DIVE TWO		
MAX DEPTHS		MDT	MAX DEPTHS		MDT
fsw	msw	minutes	fsw	msw	minutes
110	33	9	70	21	28
100	30	13	65	20	28
90	27	17	60	18	38
80	24	22	55	17	38
70	21	28	50	15	54
60	18	38	45	14	54
50	15	54	40	12	85
40	12	85	35	11	85
30	9	125	30	9	125

This table is designed for scuba dives employing air.

Read the instructions and seek proper training before using this table or compressed air. Even strict compliance with this table will not guarantee avoidance of decompression sickness.

RGBM Air Dive Table

2,000 to 6,000 ft / 610 to 1829 m

Abbreviation Key
fsw = feet seawater   msw = meters seawater   MDT = Maximum Dive Time
SIT = Surface Interval Time DCS = Decompression Sickness   fpm = feet per minute
                             mpm = meters per minute

Rules for Table Use
- Depth measuring devices may require correction for use at altitude and in fresh water to determine a diveŕs actual dive depths and ascent/descent rates.
- Find your first diveŕs maximum depth in fsw or msw in the left two columns (Dive One). Follow that row to the right to get your MDT for Dive One and continue to the next columns under Dive Two to determine permitted repetitive depth and MDT for your second dive.
- A minimum SIT of 1:30 hours is required between Dive One and Dive Two.
- If your actual dive depth is not listed, use the MDT for the next greater depth listed.
- Dive Two may be shallower, but cannot exceed depth and MDT to the immediate right and on the same row as Dive One.
- The maximum descent rate on all dives is 75 fpm (23 mpm).
- The maximum ascent rate is 30 fpm (9 mpm).
- All dives require a safety stop at about 15 fsw (5 msw) (+/- 3 feet or 1 meter) for 3 minutes.
- No more than two repetitive dives within a 12-hour period.
- After a single dive in an 18-hour period wait a minimum of 12 hours before flying or ascending to an altitude greater than 12,000 feet/3658 meters. After two dives wait 15 hours.
- Inverted depth profiles (a shallow dive followed by a deeper dive) and mandatory staged decompression dives are not permitted while using this table.
- If you accidentally exceed your MDT cease all diving activities for 24 hours. If exceeded by less than 5 minutes, conduct a decompression stop at about 15 fsw (5 msw) for 6 minutes; if exceeded by 5 to 10 minutes, stop at about 15 fsw (5 msw) for 9 minutes before surfacing.
- If symptoms of DCS manifest breathe oxygen and evacuate to the nearest recompression facility.
- Example 1: Dive 1 to 110 fsw (34 msw) for 9 minutes, followed by a 1:30 SIT: followed by Dive 2 to 70 fsw (21 msw) for 28 minutes.
- Example 2: Dive 1 to 100 fsw (30 msw) for 11 minutes followed by a 2:30 minute SIT; followed by Dive 2 to 50 (15 msw) for 40 minutes.

NAUI Worldwide Copyright © 2001. All rights reserved.

Reduced Gradient Bubble Model (RGBM)
Dive Table - Air
6,000 to 10,000 ft / 1829 to 3048 m

DIVE ONE			DIVE TWO		
MAX DEPTHS		MDT	MAX DEPTHS		MDT
fsw	msw	minutes	fsw	msw	minutes
90	27	11	60	18	28
80	24	15	55	17	28
70	21	21	50	15	40
60	18	28	45	14	40
50	15	40	40	12	64
40	12	64	35	11	64
30	9	103	30	9	103

This table is designed for scuba dives employing air.

Read the instructions and seek proper training before using this table or compressed air. Even strict compliance with this table will not guarantee avoidance of decompression sickness.

RGBM Air Dive Table
6,000 to 10,000 ft / 1829 to 3048 m

Abbreviation Key
fsw = feet seawater   msw = meters seawater   MDT = Maximum Dive Time
SIT = Surface Interval Time   DCS = Decompression Sickness   fpm = feet per minute
mpm = meters per minute

Rules for Table Use
- Depth measuring devices may require correction for use at altitude and in fresh water to determine a diverís actual dive depths and ascent/descent rates.
- Find your first diveís maximum depth in fsw or msw in the left two columns (Dive One). Follow that row to the right to get your MDT for Dive One and continue to the next columns under Dive Two to determine permitted repetitive depth and MDT for your second dive.
- A minimum SIT of 2:00 hours is required between dive one and dive two.
- If your actual dive depth is not listed, use the MDT for the next greater depth listed.
- Dive Two may be shallower, but cannot exceed depth and MDT listed to the immediate right and on the same row as Dive One.
- The maximum descent rate on all dives is 75 fpm (23 mpm).
- The maximum ascent rate is 30 fpm (9 mpm).
- All dives require a safety stop at about 15 fsw (5 msw) (+/- 3 feet or 1 meter) for 3 minutes.
- No more than two repetitive dives within a 12 hour period.
- After a single dive in an 18-hour period wait a minimum of 15 hours before flying or ascending to an altitude greater than 15,000 feet/4572 meters. After two dives wait 18 hours.
- Inverted depth profiles (a shallow dive followed by a deeper dive) and mandatory staged decompression dives are not permitted while using this table.
- If you accidentally exceed your MDT cease all diving activities for 24 hours. If exceeded by less than 5 minutes, conduct a decompression stop at about 15 fsw (5 msw) for 6 minutes; if exceeded by 5 to 10 minutes, stop at about 15 fsw (5 msw) for 9 minutes before surfacing.
- If symptoms of DCS manifest breathe oxygen and evacuate to the nearest recompression facility.
- Example 1: Dive 1 to 90 fsw (27 msw) for 11 minutes, followed by a 2:00 SIT; followed by Dive 2 to 60 fsw (18 msw) for 28 minutes.
- Example 2: Dive 1 to 75 fsw (23 msw) for 15 minutes followed by a 2:30 minute SIT; followed by Dive 2 to 45 fsm (14 msw) for 40 minutes.

NAUI Worldwide Copyright © 2001. All rights reserved.

Reduced Gradient Bubble Model (RGBM)
Dive Table - EAN 32
Sea Level to 2,000 ft / 610 m

DIVE ONE			DIVE TWO			DIVE THREE		
MAX DEPTHS		MDT	MAX DEPTHS		MDT	MAX DEPTHS		MDT
fsw	msw	minutes	fsw	msw	minutes	fsw	msw	minutes
120	36	20	80	24	47	40	12	150
110	33	25	75	23	47	40	12	150
100	30	30	70	21	60	40	12	150
90	27	38	65	20	60	40	12	150
80	24	47	60	18	85	40	12	150
70	21	60	55	17	85	40	12	150
60	18	85	50	15	115	40	12	150
50	15	115	45	14	115	40	12	150
40	12	150	40	12	150	40	12	150

This table is designed for scuba dives employing EAN 32.

Read the instructions and seek proper training before using this table or EAN 32. Even strict compliance with this table will not guarantee avoidance of decompression sickness.

RGBM EAN 32 Dive Table
Sea Level to 2,000 ft / 610 m

Abbreviation Key
fsw = feet seawater   msw = meters seawater   MDT = Maximum Dive Time
SIT = Surface Interval Time DCS = Decompression Sickness fpm= feet per minute
                           mpm= meters per minute

Rules for Table Use
- Depth measuring devices may require correction for use at altitude and in fresh water to determine a diveís actual dive depths and ascent/descent rates.
- Find your first diveís maximum depth in fsw or msw in the left two columns (Dive One). Follow that row to the right to get your MDT for Dive One and continue to the next columns under Dive Two to determine permitted repetitive depth and MDT for your second dive. Continue to the next columns under Dive Three to determine repetitive depth and MDT for your third dive.
- A minimum SIT of 1:00 hour is required between Dive One and Dive Two and Dive Three.
- If your actual dive depth is not listed, use the MDT for the next greater depth listed.
- Dive Two may be shallower, but cannot exceed depth and MDT to the immediate right and on the same row as Dive One. Dive Three may be shallower than the depth listed but may not exceed the MDT in columnthree.
- The maximum descent rate on all dives is 75 fpm (23 mpm).
- The maximum ascent rate is 30 fpm (9 mpm).
- All dives require a safety stop at about 15 fsw (5 msw) (+/- 3 feet or 1 meter) for 3 minutes.
- No more than three repetitive dives within a 12 hour period.
- After a single dive in an 18-hour period wait a minimum of 12 hours before flying or ascending to an altitude greater than 8,000 feet/2438 meters. After two dives wait 15 hours and after three dives wait 18 hours.
- Inverted depth profiles (a shallow dive followed by a deeper dive) and mandatory staged decompression dives are not permitted while using this table.
- If you accidentally exceed your MDT cease all diving activities for 24 hours. If exceeded by less than 5 minutes, conduct a decompression stop at about 15 fsw (5msw) for 6 minutes; if exceeded by 5 to 10 minutes, stop at about 15 fsw (5msw) for 9 minutes before surfacing.
- If symptoms of DCS manifest breathe oxygen and evacuate to the nearest recompression facility.
- Example 1: Dive 1 to 120 fsw (37 msw) for 20 minutes, followed by a 1:00;SIT followed by Dive 2 to 80 fsw (24 msw) for 47 minutes; followed by a 1:00 SIT; followed by Dive 3 to 40 fsw (12 msw) for 150 minutes.
- Example 2: Dive 1 to 110 fsw (33 msw) for 15 minutes followed by a 1 hour and 30 minute SIT; followed by Dive 2 to 65 fsw (20 msw) for 25 minutes; followed by a 1:45 SIT; followed by Dive 3 to 40 fsw (12 msw) for 60 minutes.

NAUI Worldwide Copyright © 2001. All rights reserved.

Reduced Gradient Bubble Model (RGBM)
Dive Table - EAN 32
2,000 to 6,000 ft / 610 to 1829 m

DIVE ONE			DIVE TWO		
MAX DEPTHS		MDT	MAX DEPTHS		MDT
fsw	msw	minutes	fsw	msw	minutes
100	30	20	65	20	43
90	27	26	60	18	57
80	24	33	55	17	57
70	21	43	50	15	84
60	18	57	45	14	84
50	15	84	40	12	120
40	12	120	35	11	120
30	9	150	30	9	150

This table is designed for scuba dives employing EAN 32.

Read the instructions and seek proper training before using this table or EAN 32. Even strict compliance with this table will not guarantee avoidance of decompression sickness.

RGBM EAN 32 Dive Tables

2,000 to 6,000 ft / 610 to 1829 m

Abbreviation Key
fsw = feet seawater   msw = meters seawater   MDT = Maximum Dive Time
SIT = Surface Interval Time   DCS = Decompression Sickness   fpm = feet per minute
                         mpm = meters per minute

Rules for Table Use
- Depth measuring devices may require correction for use at altitude and in fresh water to determine a diver's actual dive depths and ascent/descent rates.
- Find your first dive's maximum depth in fsw or msw in the left two columns (Dive One). Follow that row to the right to get your MDT for Dive One and continue to the next columns under Dive Two to determine permitted repetitive depth and MDT for your second dive.
- A minimum SIT of 1:30 hours is required between Dive One and Dive Two.
- If your actual dive depth is not listed, use the MDT for the next greater depth listed.
- Dive Two may be shallower, but cannot exceed depth and the MDT to the immediate right and on the same row as Dive One.
- The maximum descent rate on all dives is 75 fpm (23 mpm).
- The maximum ascent rate is 30 fpm (9 mpm).
- All dives require a safety stop at about 15 fsw (5 msw) (+/- 3 feet or 1 meter) for 3 minutes.
- No more than two repetitive dives within a 12-hour period.
- After a single dive in an 18-hour period wait a minimum of 12 hours before flying or ascending to an altitude greater than 12,000 feet/3658 meters. After two dives wait 15 hours.
- Inverted depth profiles (a shallow dive followed by a deeper dive) and mandatory staged decompression dives are not permitted while using this table.
- If you accidentally exceed your MDT cease all diving activities for 24 hours. If exceeded by less than 5 minutes, conduct a decompression stop at about 15 fsw (5 msw) for 6 minutes; if exceeded by 5 to 10 minutes, stop at about 15 fsw (5 msw) for 9 minutes before surfacing.
- If symptoms of DCS manifest breathe oxygen and evacuate to the nearest recompression facility.
- Example 1: Dive 1 to 100 fsw (30 msw) for 20 minutes, followed by a 1:30 SIT; followed by Dive 2 to 65 fsw (20 msw) for 43 minutes.
- Example 2: Dive 1 to 100 fsw (30 msw) for 15 minutes followed by a 2:30 minute SIT; followed by Dive 2 to 50 fsw (15 msw) for 60 minutes.

NAUI Worldwide Copyright © 2001. All right reserved.

APPENDIX

Reduced Gradient Bubble Model (RGBM)
Dive Table - EAN 32
6,000 to 10,000 ft / 1829 to 3048m

DIVE ONE			DIVE TWO		
MAX DEPTHS		MDT	MAX DEPTHS		MDT
fsw	msw	minutes	fsw	msw	minutes
90	27	17	60	18	43
80	24	24	55	17	43
70	21	32	50	15	60
60	18	43	45	14	60
50	15	60	40	12	96
40	12	96	35	11	96
30	9	140	30	9	140

This table is designed for scuba dives employing EAN 32.

Read the instructions and seek proper training before using this table or EAN 32. Even strict compliance with this table will not guarantee avoidance of decompression sickness.

RGBM EAN 32 Dive Table

6,000 to 10,000 ft / 1829 to 3048 m

Abbreviation Key
fsw = feet seawater
SIT = Surface Interval Time
msw = meters seawater
DCS = Decompression Sickness
mpm= meters per minute
MDT = Maximum Dive Time
fpm= feet per minute

Rules for Table Use
- Depth measuring devices may require correction for use at altitude and in fresh water to determine a diverís actual dive depths and ascent/descent rates.
- Find your first dive is maximum depth in fsw or msw in the left two columns (Dive One). Follow that row to the right to get your MDT for Dive One and continue to the next columns under Dive Two to determine permitted repetitive depth and MDT for your second dive.
- A minimum SIT of 2:00 hours is required between Dive One and Dive Two.
- If your actual dive depth is not listed, use the MDT for the next greater depth listed.
- Dive Two may be shallower, but cannot exceed depth and MDT to the immediate right and on the same row as Dive One.
- The maximum descent rate on all dives is 75 fpm (23 mpm).
- The maximum ascent rate is 30 fpm (9 mpm).
- All dives require a safety stop at about 15 fsw (5 msw) (+/- 3 feet or 1 meter) for 3 minutes.
- No more than two repetitive dives within a 12-hour period.
- After a single dive in an 18-hour period wait a minimum of 15 hours before flying or ascending to an altitude greater than 15,000 feet/4572 meters. After two dives wait 18 hours.
- Inverted depth profiles (a shallow dive followed by a deeper dive) and mandatory staged decompression dives are not permitted.
- If you accidentally exceed your MDT cease all diving activities for 24 hours. If exceeded by less than 5 minutes, conduct a decompression stop at about 15 fsw (5 msw) for 6 minutes; if exceeded by 5 to 10 minutes, stop at about 15 fsw (5 msw) for 9 minutes before surfacing.
- If symptoms of DCS manifest breathe oxygen and evacuate to the nearest recompression facility.
- Example 1: Dive 1 to 90 fsw (27 msw) for 17 minutes, followed by a 2:00 SIT; followed by Dive 2 to 60 fsw (18 msw) for 43 minutes.
- Example 2: Dive 1 to 75 fsw (23 msw) for 20 minutes followed by a 2:30 minute SIT; followed by Dive 2 to 45 fsw (14 msw) for 50 minutes.

NAUI Worldwide Copyright © 2001. All rights reserved.

Reduced Gradient Bubble Model (RGBM)
Dive Table - EAN 36
Sea Level to 2,000 ft / 610 m

DIVE ONE			DIVE TWO			DIVE THREE		
MAX DEPTHS		MDT	MAX DEPTHS		MDT	MAX DEPTHS		MDT
fsw	msw	minutes	fsw	msw	minutes	fsw	msw	minutes
110	33	31	80	23	60	50	15	150
100	30	35	75	21	60	50	15	150
90	27	46	70	20	85	50	15	150
80	24	60	65	18	85	50	15	150
70	21	85	60	17	115	50	15	150
60	18	115	55	15	115	50	15	150
50	15	150	50	14	150	50	15	150

This table is designed for scuba dives employing EAN 36.

Read the instructions and seek proper training before using this table or EAN 36. Even strict compliance with this table will not guarantee avoidance of decompression sickness.

RGBM EAN 36 Dive Table
Sea Level to 2,000 ft / 610 m

Abbreviation Key
fsw = feet seawater   msw = meters seawater   MDT = Maximum Dive Time
SIT = Surface Interval Time DCS = Decompression Sickness fpm = feet per minute
                             mpm = meters per minute

Rules for Table Use
- Depth measuring devices may require correction for use at altitude and in fresh water to determine a diver's actual dive depths and ascent/descent rates.
- Find your first dive is maximum depth in fsw or msw in the left two columns (Dive One). Follow that row to the right to get your MDT for Dive One and continue to the next columns under Dive Two to determine permitted repetitive depth and MDT for your second dive. Continue to the next columns under Dive Three to determine repetitive depth and MDT for your third dive.
- A minimum SIT of 1:00 hour is required between Dive One and Dive Two and Dive Three.
- If your actual dive depth is not listed, use the MDT for the next greater depth listed.
- Dive Two may be shallower, but cannot exceed depth and MDT to the immediate right and on the same row as Dive One. Dive Three may be shallower than the depth listed but may not exceed the MDT in column three.
- The maximum descent rate on all dives is 75 fpm (23 mpm).
- The maximum ascent rate is 30 fpm (9 mpm).
- All dives require a safety stop at about 15 fsw (5 msw) (+/- 3 feet or 1 meter) for 3 minutes.
- No more than three repetitive dives within a 12-hour period.
- After a single dive in an 18-hour period wait a minimum of 12 hours before flying or ascending to an altitude greater than 8,000 feet/2438 meters. After two dives wait 15 hours and after three dives wait 18 hours.
- Inverted depth profiles (a shallow dive followed by a deeper dive) and mandatory staged decompression dives are not permitted while using this table.
- If you accidentally exceed your MDT cease all diving activities for 24 hours. If exceeded by less than 5 minutes, conduct a decompression stop at about 15 fsw (5 msw) for 6 minutes; if exceeded by 5 to 10 minutes, stop at about 15 fsw (5 msw) for 9 minutes before surfacing.
- If symptoms of DCS manifest breathe oxygen and evacuate to the nearest recompression facility.
- Example 1: Dive 1 to 110 fsw (34 m) for 31 minutes, followed by a 1:00 SIT; followed by Dive 2 to 80 fsw (24 msw) for 60 minutes; followed by a 1:00 SIT; followed by Dive 3 to 50 fsw (15 msw) for 150 minutes.
- Example 2: Dive 1 to 105 fsw (32 msw) for 20 minutes followed by a 1 hour and 30 minute SIT; followed by Dive 2 to 71 fsw (22 msw) for 55 minutes; followed by a 1:45 SIT; followed by Dive 3 to 40 fsw (12 msw) for 60 minutes.

NAUI Worldwide Copyright © 2001. All rights reserved.

APPENDIX

Reduced Gradient Bubble Model (RGBM)
Dive Table - EAN 36
2,000 to 6,000 ft / 610 to 1829 m

DIVE SAFETY THROUGH EDUCATION

DIVE ONE			DIVE TWO		
MAX DEPTHS		MDT	MAX DEPTHS		MDT
fsw	msw	minutes	fsw	msw	minutes
90	27	21	60	18	79
80	24	39	55	17	79
70	21	54	50	15	114
60	18	79	45	14	114
50	15	114	40	12	150
40	12	150	35	11	150
30	9	150	30	9	150

This table is designed for scuba dives employing EAN 36.

Read the instructions and seek proper training before using this table or EAN 36. Even strict compliance with this table will not guarantee avoidance of decompression sickness.

RGBM EAN 36 Dive Table

2,000 to 6,000 ft / 610 to 1829 m

Abbreviation Key
fsw = feet seawater msw = meters seawater MDT = Maximum Dive Time
SIT = Surface Interval Time DCS = Decompression Sickness fpm= feet per minute
  mpm= Meters per minute

Rules for Table Use
- Depth measuring devices may require correction for use at altitude and in fresh water to determine a diverís actual dive depths and ascent/descent rates.
- Find your first dive is maximum depth in fsw or msw in the left two columns (Dive One). Follow that row to the right to get your MDT for Dive One and continue to the next columns under Dive Two to determine permitted repetitive depth and MDT for your second dive.
- A minimum SIT of 1:30 hours is required between Dive One and Dive Two.
- If your actual dive depth is not listed, use the MDT for the next greater depth listed.
- Dive Two may be shallower, but cannot exceed depth and MDT listed to the immediate right and on the same row as Dive One.
- The maximum descent rate on all dives is 75 fpm (23 mpm).
- The maximum ascent rate is 30 fpm (9 mpm).
- All dives require a safety stop at about 15 fsw (5 msw) (+/- 3 feet or 1 meter) for 3 minutes.
- No more than two repetitive dives within a 12-hour period.
- After a single dive in an 18-hour period wait a minimum of 12 hours before flying or ascending to an altitude greater than 12,000 feet/3658 meters. After two dives wait 15 hours.
- Inverted depth profiles (a shallow dive followed by a deeper dive) and mandatory staged decompression dives are not permitted while using this table.
- If you accidentally exceed your MDT cease all diving activities for 24 hours. If exceeded by less than 5 minutes, conduct a decompression stop at about 15 fsw (5 msw) for 6 minutes; if exceeded by 5 to 10 minutes, stop at about 15 fsw (5 msw) for 9 minutes before surfacing.
- If symptoms of DCS manifest breathe oxygen and evacuate to the nearest recompression facility.
- Example 1: Dive 1 to 90 fsw (27 msw) for 31 minutes, followed by a 1:30 SIT; followed by Dive 2 to 60 fsw (18 msw) for 79 minutes.
- Example 2: Dive 1 to 75 fsw (23 msw) for 30 minutes followed by a 2:30 minute SIT; followed by Dive 2 to 45 (14 msw) for 60 minutes.

NAUI Worldwide Copyright © 2001. All rights reserved.

Reduced Gradient Bubble Model (RGBM)
Dive Table - EAN 36
6,000 to 10,000 ft / 1829 to 3048 m

DIVE ONE			DIVE TWO		
MAX DEPTHS		MDT	MAX DEPTHS		MDT
fsw	msw	minutes	fsw	msw	minutes
80	24	29	55	17	54
70	21	37	50	15	84
60	18	54	45	14	84
50	15	84	40	12	128
40	12	128	35	11	128
30	9	150	30	9	150

This table is designed for scuba dives employing EAN 36.

Read the instructions and seek proper training before using this table or EAN 36. Even strict compliance with this table will not guarantee avoidance of decompression sickness.

RGBM EAN 36 Dive Table

6,000 to 10,000 ft /1829 to 3048 m

Abbreviation Key:
fsw = feet seawater   msw = meters seawater   MDT =Maximum Dive Time
SIT = Surface Interval Time   DCS = Decompression Sickness   fpm = feet per minute
    mpm = meters per minute

Rules for Table Use
- Depth measuring devices may require correction for use at altitude and in fresh water to determine a diver's actual dive depths and ascent/descent rates.
- Find your first dive's maximum depth in fsw or msw in the left two columns (Dive One). Follow that row to the right to get your MDT for Dive One and continue to the next columns under Dive Two to determine permitted repetitive depth and MDT for your second dive.
- A minimum SIT of 2:00 hours is required between Dive One and Dive Two.
- If your actual dive depth is not listed, use the MDT for the next greater depth listed.
- Dive Two may be shallower, but cannot exceed the depth and MDT to the immediate right and on the same row as Dive One.
- The maximum descent rate on all dives is 75 fpm (23 mpm).
- The maximum ascent rate is 30 fpm (9 mpm).
- All dives require a safety stop at about 15 fsw (5 msw) (+/- 3 feet or 1 meter) for 3 minutes.
- No more than two repetitive dives within a 12-hour period.
- After a single dive in an 18-hour period wait a minimum of 15 hours before flying or ascending to an altitude greater than 15,000 feet/4572 meters. After two dives wait 18 hours.
- Inverted depth profiles (a shallow dive followed by a deeper dive) and mandatory staged decompression dives are not permitted while using this table.
- If you accidentally exceed your MDT cease all diving activities for 24 hours. If exceeded by less than 5 minutes, conduct a decompression stop at about 15 fsw (5 msw) for 6 minutes; if exceeded by 5 to 10 minutes, stop at about 15 fsw (5 msw) for 9 minutes before surfacing.
- If symptoms of DCS manifest breathe oxygen and evacuate to the nearest recompression facility.
- Example 1: Dive 1 to 80 fsw (24 msw) for 29 minutes, followed by a 2:00 SIT; followed by Dive 2 to 55 fsw (17 msw) for 54 minutes.
- Example 2: Dive 1 to 75 fsw (23 msw) for 20 minutes followed by a 2:30 minute SIT; followed by Dive 2 to 45 (14 msw) for 60 minutes.

NAUI Worldwide Copyright © 2001. All rights reserved.

· REFERENCES ·

Adamson A.W., 1976, *The Physical Chemistry of Surfaces*, New York: John Wiley and Sons.

Batchelor G.K., 1953, *Theory of Homogeneous Turbulence*, New York: Cambridge University Press.

Bateman J.B. and Lang J., 1945, "Formation and Growth of Bubbles in Aqueous Solutions," *Canada. J. Res.* E23, 22-31.

Behnke A.R., 1967, "The Isobaric (Oxygen Window) Principle of Decompression," *Trans. Third Annual Conf. Marine Tech, Soc.* 1, 213-228.

Behnke A.R., 1945, "Decompression Sickness Incident to Deep Sea Diving and High Altitude," *Medicine* 24, 381-402.

Bennett P.B. and Elliot D.H., 1996, *The Physiology and Medicine of Diving and Compressed Air Work*, London: Bailiere Tindall and Cassell.

Berghage T.E. and Durman D., 1980, "US Navy Air Recompression Schedule Risk Analysis," *Nav. Med. Res. Bull.* 1, 1-22.

Boycott A.E., Damant G.C.C., and Haldane J.S., 1908, "The Prevention of Compressed Air Illness," *J. Hyg.* 8, 342-443.

Bozanic J., 2002, *Mastering Rebreathers*, Flagstaff: Best.

Buckles R.G., 1968, "The Physics of Bubble Formation and Growth," *Aerospace Med.* 39, 1062-1069.

Buhlmann A.A., 1984, *Decompression/Decompression Sickness*, Berlin: Springer Verlag.

Conkin J. and Van Liew H.D., 1991, "Failure of the Straight Line Boundary Between Safe and Unsafe Decompressions When Extraoplated to the Hypobaric Regime," *Undersea Biomed. Res.* 18, 16.

Des Granges M., 1957, "Repetitive Diving Decompression Tables," *USN Experimental Diving Unit Report*, NEDU 6-57, Washington D.C.

Duffner G.J., Synder J.F., and Smith L.L., 1959, "Adaptation of Helium-Oxygen to Mixed Gas Scuba," *USN Experimental Diving Unit Report*, NEDU 3-59, Washington, D.C.

Dwyer J.V., 1956, "Calculation of Repetitive Diving Decompression Tables," *USN Experimental Diving Unit Report*, NEDU 1-57, Washington D.C.

Eckenhoff R.G., Olstad C.E., Parker S.F., and Bondi K.R., 1986, "Direct Ascent from Shallow Air Saturation Exposures," *Undersea Biomed. Res.* 13, 305-316.

Epstein P.S. and Plesset M.S., 1950, "On the Stability of Gas Bubbles in Liquid-Gas Solutions," *J. Chm. Phys.* 18, 1505-1509.

Evans A. and Walder D.N., 1969, "Significance of Gas Macronuclei in the Aetiology of Decompression Sickness," *Nature London* 222, 251-252.

Fisher J.C., 1948, "The Fracture of Liquids," *J. Appl. Phys.* 19, 1062-1067.

Frenkel J., 1946, *Kinetic Theory of Liquids*, New York: Oxford University Press.

Gernhardt M.L., Lambertsen C.J., Miller R.G., and Hopkins E., 1990, "Evaluation of a Theoretical Model of Tissue Gas Phase Growth and Resolution During Decompression from Air Diving," *Undersea Biomed. Res.* 17, 95.

Hamilton R.W., 1975, "Development of Decompression Procedures for Depths in Excess of 400 Feet," *Undersea and Hyperbaric Medical Society Report*, WS: 2-28-76, Bethesda.

Harvey E.N., Barnes D.K., McElroy W.D., Whiteley A.H., Pease D.C., and Cooper K.W., 1944, "Bubble Formation in Animals. I. Physical Factors," *J. Cell. Comp. Physiol.* 24, 1-22.

Harvey E.N., Whiteley A.H., McElroy W.D., Pease D.C., and Barnes D.K., 1944, "Bubble Formation in Animals. II. Gas Nuclei and Their Distribution in Blood and Tissues," *J. Cell Comp. Physiol.* 24, 23-24.

Harvey E.N., McElroy W.D., Whiteley A.H., Warren G.H., and Pease D.C., 1944, "Bubble Formation in Animals. III. An Analysis of Gas Tension and Hydrostatic Pressure in Cats," *J. Cell. Comp. Physiol.* 24, 117-132.

Hempleman H.V., 1957, "Further Basic Facts on Decompression Sickness, Investigation into the Decompression Tables," *Medical Research Council Report*, UPS 168, London.

Hempleman H.V., 1952, "A New Theoretical Basis for the Calculation of Decompression Tables," *Medical Research Council Report*, UPS 131, London.

Hennessy T.R. and Hempleman H.V., 1977, "An Examination of the Critical Released Gas Concept in Decompression Sickness," *Proc. Royal Soc.* London B197, 299-313.

Hennessy T.R., 1974, "The Interaction of Diffusion and Perfusion in Homogeneous Tissue," *Bull. Math. Biol.* 36, 505-527.

Hills B.A., 1977, *Decompression Sickness*, New York: John Wiley and Sons.

Hills B.A., 1968, "Variation in Susceptibility to Decompression Sickness," *Int. J. Biometeor.* 12, 343-349.

Hills B.A., 1968, "Relevant Phase Conditions for Predicting the Occurrence of Decompression Sickness," *J. Appl. Physiol.* 25, 310-315.

Hirschfelder J.O., Curtiss C.F., and Bird R.B., 1964, *Molecular Theory of Gases and Liquids*, New York: John Wiley and Sons.

Keller H. and Buhlmann A.A., 1965, "Deep Diving and Short Decompression by Breathing Mixed Gases," *J. Appl. Physiol.* 20, 1267.

REFERENCES

Kunkle T.D. and Beckman E.L., 1983, "Bubble Dissolution Physics and the Treatment of Decompression Sickness," *Med. Phys.* 10, 184-190.

Lambertsen J.L. and Bornmann R.C., 1979, *Isobaric Inert Gas Counterdiffusion*, Undersea and Hyperbaric Medical Society Publication 54WS(IC)1-11-82, Bethesda.

Lang M.A. and Vann R.D., 1992, *Proceedings of the American Academy of Underwater Sciences Repetitive Diving Workshop*, AAUS Safety Publication AAUSDSP-RDW-02-92, Costa Mesa.

Lang M.A. and Egstrom G.H., 1990, *Proceedings of the American Academy of Underwater Sciences Biomechanics of Safe Ascents Workshop*, American Academy of Underwater Sciences Diving Safety Publication, AAUSDSP-BSA-01-90, Costa Mesa.

Lang M.A. and Hamilton R.W., 1989, *Proceedings of the American Academy of Underwater Sciences Dive Computer Workshop*, University of Southern California Sea Grant Publication, USCSG-TR-01-89, Los Angeles.

Lehner C.E., Hei D.J., Palta M., Lightfoot E.N., and Lanphier E.H., 1988, "Accelerated Onset of Decompression Sickness in Sheep after Short Deep Dives," *University of Wisconsin Sea Grant College Program Report*, WIS-SG-88-843, Madison.

Leitch D.R. and Barnard E.E.P., 1982, "Observations on No Stop and Repetitive Air and Oxynitrogen Diving," *Undersea Biomed. Res.* 9, 113-129.

Le Messurier D.H. and Hills B.A., 1965, *Decompression Sickness: A Study of Diving Techniques in the Torres Strait*, Hvaldradets Skrifter 48, 54-84.

Lenihan D., 2002, *Submerged*, New York: Newmarket Press.

Neuman T.S., Hall D.A., and Linaweaver P.G., 1976, "Gas Phase Separation During Decompression in Man," *Undersea Biomed. Res.* 7, 107-112.

Nishi R.Y., Eatock B.C., Buckingham I.P., and Ridgewell B.A., 1982, "Assessment of Decompression Profiles by Ultrasonic Monitoring: No Decompression Dives," *Defense and Civil Institute of Environmental Medicine Report*, D.C.IEM 82-R-38, Toronto.

Pease D.C. and Blinks L.R., 1947, "Cavitation from Solid Surfaces in the Absence of Gas Nuclei," *J. Phys. Coll. Chem.* 51, 556-567.

Pilmanis A.A., 1976, "Intravenous Gas Emboli in Man after Compressed Air Ocean Diving," *Office of Naval Research Contract Report*, N00014-67-A-0269-0026, Washington, D.C.

Powell M.R., Waligora J.M., Kumar K.V., Robinson R., and Butler B., 1995, "Modifications of Physiological Processes Concerning Extravehicular Activity in Microgravity," *Engineering Society for Advanced Mobility Land Sea and Space International Technical Series Report* 951590, Warrendale.

Powell M.R., Waligora J.M., Norfleet W.T., and Kumar K.V., 1993, "Project ARGO — Gas Phase Formation in Simulated Microgravity," *NASA Technical Memo* 104762, Houston.

Powell M.R., 1991, "Doppler Indices of Gas Phase Formation in Hypobaric Environments: Time Intensity Analysis," *NASA Technical Memo* 102176, Houston.

Sawatzky K.D. and Nishi R.Y., 1990, "Intravascular Doppler Detected Bubbles and Decompression Sickness," *Undersea Biomed. Res.* 17, 34-39.

Schreiner H.R. and Hamilton R.W., 1987, *Validation of Decompression Tables*, Undersea and Hyperbaric Medical Society Publication 74 (VAL), Bethesda.

Sears, F.W., 1969, *Thermodynamics*, Reading: Addison Wesley.

Sheffield P.J., 1990, *Flying after Diving*, Undersea and Hyperbaric Medical Society Publication 77 (FLYDIV), Bethesda.

Smith K.H. and Stayton L., 1978, "Hyperbaric Decompression by Means of Bubble Detection," *Office of Naval Research Report*, N0001-469-C-0402, Washington D.C.

Spencer M.P., 1976, "Decompression Limits for Compressed Air Determined by Ultrasonically Detected Blood Bubbles," *J. Appl. Physiol.* 40, 229-235.

Spencer M.P. and Campbell S.D., 1968, "The Development of Bubbles in the Venous and Arterial Blood During Hyperbaric Decompression," *Bull. Mason Cli.* 22, 26-32.

Strauss R.H. and Kunkle T.D., 1974, "Isobaric Bubble Growth: Consequence of Altering Atmospheric Gas," *Science* 186, 443-444.

Tikuisis P., 1986, "Modeling the Observations of *In Vivo* Bubble Formation with Hydrophobic Crevices," *Undersea Biomed. Res* 13, 165-180.

Tikuisis P., Ward C.A., and Venter R.D., 1983, "Bubble Evolution in a Stirred Volume of Liquid Closed to Mass Transport," *J. Appl. Phys.* 54, 1-9.

Van Liew H.D. and Hlastala M.P., 1969, "Influence of Bubble Size and Blood Perfusion on Absorption of Gas Bubbles in Tissues," *Resp. Physiol.* 24, 111-121.

Van Liew H.D., Bishop B., Walder P.D., and Rahn H., 1975, "Bubble Growth and Mechanical Properties of Tissue in Decompression," *Undersea Biomed. Res.* 2, 185 194.

Vann R.D., Grimstad J., and Nielsen C.H., 1980, "Evidence for Gas Nuclei in Decompressed Rats," *Undersea Biomed. Res.* 7, 107-112.

Vann R.D. and Clark H.G., 1975, "Bubble Growth and Mechanical Properties of Tissue in Decompression," *Undersea Biomed. Res.* 2, 185-194.

Walder D.N., Evans A., and Hempleman H.V., 1968, "Ultrasonic Monitoring of Decompression," *Lancet.* 1, 897-898.

Walder D.N., 1968, "Adaptation to Decompression Sickness in Caisson Work," *Biometeor.* 11, 350-359.

Weathersby P.K., Survanshi S., and Homer L.D., 1985, "Statistically Based Decompression Tables: Analysis of Standard Air Dives, 1950-1970," *Naval Medical Research Institute Report*, NMRI 85-16, Bethesda.

Weathersby P.K., Homer L.D., and Flynn E.T., 1984, "On the Likelihood of Decompression Sickness," *J. Appl. Physiol.* 57, 815-825.

Wienke B.R., 2001, *Technical Diving in Depth*, Flagstaff: Best.

Wienke B.R., 1994, *Basic Diving Physics and Application*, Flagstaff: Best.

Wienke B.R., 1992, "Numerical Phase Algorithm for Decompression Computers and Application," *Comp. Biol. Med.* 22, 389-406.

Wienke B.R., 1991, *Basic Decompression Theory and Application*, Flagstaff: Best.

Wienke B.R., 1991, "Bubble Number Saturation Curve and Asymptotics of Hypobaric and Hyperbaric Exposures," *Int. J. Biomed. Comp.* 29, 215-225.

Wienke B.R., 1991, *High Altitude Diving*, National Association of Underwater Instructors Technical Publication, Montclair.

Wienke B.R., 1990, "Reduced Gradient Bubble Model," *Int. J. Biomed. Comp.* 26, 237-256.

Wienke B.R., 1990, "Modeling Dissolved and Free Phase Gas Dynamics Under Decompression," *Int. J. BioMed. Comp.* 25, 193-205.

Wienke B.R., 1989, "Equivalent Multitissue and Thermodynamic Decompression Algorithms," *Int. J. BioMed. Comp.* 24, 227-245.

Wienke B.R., 1989, "Tissue Gas Exchange Models and Decompression Computations: A Review," *Undersea Biomed. Res.* 16, 53-89.

Wienke B.R., 1989, "N_2 Transfer and Critical Pressures in Tissue Compartments," *Math. Comp. Model.* 12, 1-15.

Wienke B.R., 1987, "Computational Decompression Models," *Int. J. BioMed. Comp.* 21, 205-221.

Wienke B.R., 1986, "DECOMP: Computational Package for Nitrogen Transport Modeling in Tissues," *Comp. Phys. Comm.* 40, 327-336.

Wittenborn A.F., 1963, "An Analytic Development of a Decompression Computer," *Proc. Second Symp. Underwater Physiol.*, Washington, D.C.: National Academy of Science 1, 82-90.

Workman R.D., 1965, "Calculation of Decompression Schedules for Nitrogen-Oxygen and Helium-Oxygen Dives," *USN Experimental Diving Unit Report*, NEDU 6-65, Washington D.C.

Yang W.J., 1971, "Dynamics of Gas Bubbles in Whole Blood and Plasma," *J. Biomech.* 4, 119-125.

Yount D.E. and Hoffman D.C., 1986, "On the Use of a Bubble Formation Model to Calculate Diving Tables," *Aviat. Space Environ. Med.* 57, 149-156.

Yount D.E., Gillary E.W., and Hoffman D.C., 1984, "A Microscopic Investigation of Bubble Formation Nuclei," *J. Acoust. Soc. Am.* 76, 1511-1521.

Yount D.E., 1982, "On the Evolution, Generation, and Regeneration of Gas Cavitation Nuclei," *J. Acoust. Soc. Am.* 71, 1473-1481.

Yount D.E., 1979, "Skins of Varying Permeability: A Stabilization Mechanism for Gas Cavitation Nuclei," *J. Acoust. Soc. Am.* 65, 1431-1439.

· INDEX ·

A
Abysmal diving 4
ABYSS 1, 7-8, 29, 71, 75
ABYSS/RGBM 4-5
acclimatization 17
adhesional forces 17
air 33, 70
altitude 4-5, 71
ambiphillic 19
Andrea Doria 72
aqueous 4, 12, 32, 53, 73
arterial 8-9
ascent rates 3

B
bends depth 64
bends symptoms 6
Boyle 24-26
Boyle's law 12, 22-23
bubble 8-9, 11-16, 31, 47, 57, 59, 62, 64
    distributions 73
    dynamics 3, 6
    factors 15, 74
    formation 6
    gas diffusion 9-10
    growth 2, 20, 28, 74
    models 2, 61
    numbers 28
    parameters 35
    pressure balance 10
    pressure gradient 12
    radius 22, 25
    seed 17
    theories 6
    volume 25
Buhlmann 33

C
capillary walls 14
carbon dioxide 7-8
cavitation 2
CCDT 50, 52
chamber tests 3
chokes 14

CNS 14, 63
coalescence 6
COBRA 4
cohesive forces 17
colloidal constant 26
computational algorithms 6
critical 10
    parameters 35, 39
    radius 24
    tension 13, 46
cross correction 71
cubical expansion 20

D
Dacor 15
DAN 62, 72
DCS 1, 12, 40, 59, 62, 71
de novo 8
decompression schedule 60
deep spike 4
deep stops 4, 5, 33, 44, 56-59, 62, 64
deformation 6
deterministic models 2
diffusion 2, 7-9
discontinuities 17
dissolved 2, 6, 9, 57
dissolved gas 3-4, 16, 53, 59, 75
dissolved phase elimination 6
Dive Table (AIR) 77
Dive Table (EAN 32) 77
Dive Table (EAN 36) 77
Doppler 11-12, 15, 37, 61, 72, 74
    bubble 37
    techniques 14
DPlan 44, 46
dual phase 59
    mechanics 3
    models 60
    principles 5
Duke 71
dynamics 57

E

electron micrographs 14
EOS 12-13, 15, 22-23, 53
excitation 6
excitation radius 26, 31, 43
EXPLORER 4, 29
extravascular 9

F

film 11-12
film layer 18
fluid flow 2
fluid shifts 2
folded algorithm 29
folded RGBM 33, 74
free 6, 75
    gas 2
    phase elimination 6

G

GAP 1, 7-8, 29, 75
gas
    diffusion 4, 13, 17, 29, 73
    diffusivity 25
    phases 5
    switches 53
    tension 25
gel 23, 26, 47
Gerth 62
Gibbs free energy 18
gradient factor (GF) 44, 46-47
gradients 2
Graham's law 38
growth 6
GUE 44

H

Haldane 3, 6, 15, 29, 33, 40, 44, 46-48,
    56-57, 59, 74
halftimes 7, 34
Hans Keller 63
heavy-to-light switches 64
heliair 43
heliox 33, 35, 50
helium 5, 11, 26, 31, 37-38, 43-45, 56,
    62-64, 66, 73, 75
helium myth 58

Hydrospace 1, 4, 7-8, 29, 74
hyperbaric 59
hyperbaric chambers 57
hypobaric 59

I

impermeable 24
incidence rate 53
inherent unsaturation 8, 31
intravascular 9
isobaric switches 4
isothermal compressibility 20

L

LANL 5, 63-64
Laplace 19
Levenberg-Marquardt 67
light-to-heavy gas switches 64
lipid 4, 12, 32, 53, 73
long range interactions 19

M

M-value 15, 33, 57
Mares 1, 4, 7-8, 15
mass transfer coefficient 13
mass transport coefficients 31
material dynamics 17, 24
material properties 26
maximum likelihood 37, 66
MBD 65
metabolic oxygen consumption 7
micelles 20
minimum bends depths 43
mixed gas 5
mixed gas decompression meter 5
modified and iterative RGBM 29
multiday 16, 29, 36-37, 40
multidiving 5, 15, 27-28, 38, 40
    fraction 27
    weighting 36
multiple switches 44

N

NAUI 1, 3-5, 42, 63-64, 67-68, 71-72, 74
NDLs 63, 65
nerve deformation 9

nitrogen 11, 31, 37-38, 43-45, 47, 63, 65-66, 73
nitrox 4, 33, 35-37, 50, 56, 70
nonstop air diving 40
nonstop time limits 3, 15
nucleation 2, 6
nucleation sites 6
number distribution 22

O

occlusion 6
oxygen 11, 43, 47, 52, 73
oxygen window 8

P

PADI 67-68
perfusion 2, 7-8
permeable 12, 23
persistence time 73
phase
    algorithm 4
    function 27, 28
    models 2-3, 53
    separation 2, 74
    volume 15-17, 25, 29
physical adaptation 16
physiological adaptation 16
Plexus 1, 4, 8
polyatomic structures 19
Project Dive Exploration 71
pulmonary filters 9

R

radial diffusion 26, 31
radius 10
random number generator 67
rate coefficients 73
rate constant 7
recreational diving 67
reduced gradient bubble model.
    See RGBM
reduction factors 35-37
repetitive 16, 36
reverse profile 4, 16, 28, 36, 37, 48
RGBM 3, 61, 71-74
    Data Bank 1, 70, 75
    motivation 3
    Tables 1, 4-5, 53
    underpinnings 5

risk 1, 40, 68
    analysis 70
    estimator 66

S

safety stops 3
saturation depth 64
SEALs 11
seed radii 30
separated 9
separated phase 17, 29
silent bubbles 6
size distribution 11, 13, 14
slow ascent rates 56
slow tissue compartments 13
solubilities 64
Spencer 15
Spencer limits 40
stabilization 6
statistical models 2
STINGER 4
structured fluids 19
supersaturation 2, 6, 21, 24
    gradient 73
    models 2
    ratio 66
surface tension 9, 12, 17-18, 20, 24-25
surfactant 8, 12-13, 19-20, 73
Suunto 1, 4, 7-8, 15

T

TDI 72
temperature 11-12, 18, 20-22, 25
thermal coefficient 21
thermodynamic
    energy 20
    laws 9
    model 61
thermodynamic model 56
Tiny Bubble Group 5
tissue
    bubble diffusion model 32, 61
    compartments 6, 14, 74
    halftime 33, 38, 43
    tensions 33
transfer equation 13
tribonucleation 73
trimix 33, 35, 38-39, 43-44, 46-47, 50, 53, 56
TWA 200 11

U

U.S. Navy *(see also* USN) 62, 67, 72
ultrasound imaging 61
unsaturation 8
USN *(see also* U.S. Navy) 44, 62, 67, 72

V

validation 3
variable gradients 15
varying permeability model (VPM) 5, 32, 61
venous 8-9
venous gas emboli (VGE) 14, 12
virial coefficients 26, 32
virial constants 23
VPM *(see also* varying permeability model) 15
VYTEC 4, 72

W

water vapor 8
WKPP 53, 57-59, 63-64, 72
Workman 33

YZ

Young 19
Zeagle 1, 4, 7-8
zero supersaturation 8
ZHL 33, 35, 40, 42-44, 48, 68